CHANTING
the PSALMS

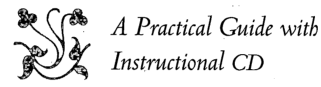

A Practical Guide with
Instructional CD

CYNTHIA BOURGEAULT

NEW SEEDS
Boston & London
2006

New Seeds Books
An imprint of Shambhala Publications, Inc.
Horticultural Hall
300 Massachusetts Avenue
Boston, Massachusetts 02115
www.newseedsbooks.com

© 2006 Cynthia Bourgeault

9 8 7 6 5 4 3 2 1

First Edition

Designed by Lora Zorian

Printed in the United States of America

⊗ This edition is printed on acid-free paper that meets
the American National Standards Institute Z39.48 Standard.
Distributed in the United States by Random House, Inc.,
and in Canada by Random House of Canada Ltd

The Library of Congress Cataloging-in-Publication Data
Bourgeault, Cynthia.
Chanting the Psalms: a practical guide with instructional CD/
Cynthia Bourgeault.
p. cm.
Includes bibliographical references and index.
ISBN-13: 978-1-59030-257-6 (hardcover: alk. paper)
ISBN-10: 1-59030-257-5
1. Bible. O.T. Psalms. 2. Chants.
3. Psalms (Music) 4. Worship.
I. Title.
BS1430.55.B68 2006
7782.2'94—dc22
2006013450

To Calvin L. Bourgeault
With gratitude and love always
Thank you for the music . . .

Contents

Preface

DURING THE PAST FOUR DECADES of Christian contemplative reawakening, contemporary seekers have been happily discovering spiritual treasures formerly locked in the coffers of cloistered monasticism. Contemplative prayer, once regarded as the pinnacle of monastic attainment, is now practiced daily by tens of thousands of Christians worldwide through simplified methods such as Centering Prayer and Christian Meditation. Lectio divina, the traditional Benedictine method of praying the scripture, has also been enjoying a popular lay revival. Even the practice of mindful work (the "labora" part of Saint Benedict's famous formula *ora et labora*) finds willing reception among modern spiritual seekers, especially veterans of ashrams and Zen centers, who understand work or "karma yoga" as a meaningful and necessary way of practicing mindfulness and compassionate service.

But chanting the psalms? For some reason, this centerpiece of the classic monastic path has been slow to migrate beyond the walls of the monastery. While the practice is much appreciated by people on retreat, even there the logistics may seem a bit intimidating. How do you find your way around the service book? What are all those little squiggles above the words that mysteriously translate into musical melodies? Don't you have to be musically trained to be able to chant? The thought of bringing monastic psalmody into your home, as a practice you might incorporate into your own daily spiritual routine, may understandably feel a bit daunt-ing. This book will show you how you can do it—and why you should.

The "why" part is actually quite straightforward. For Christians on a path of inner transformation, the psalms have traditionally been a non-negotiable cornerstone. Saint Romuald, the eleventh-century founder of the Camaldolese Benedictine order, put the matter in no uncertain terms: "The path you must follow is the psalms—never leave it." For two thou-sand years they have been the backbone of the monastic program of spir-itual awakening. Your favorite spiritual heroes have all chanted the psalms, from desert fathers such as Evagrius and John Cassian; to medieval saints and mystics such as Saint Benedict, Saint Bernard, Saint Francis, and Saint Teresa; and on into our own day, with contemplatives such as Thomas Merton, Thomas Keating, and Joan Chittister. If you want to take this tradition all the way back to bedrock, you'll find yourself face-to-face with Jesus, who chanted the psalms as the native language of his own spir-itual yearning.

So at the very least, there is a powerful lineage behind this practice. And yes, while it may be an unconscious lineage, simply the force of tra-dition and habit, the argument I will make in this book is that it is, in fact, a conscious lineage. The psalms have an intentional and effective part to play in fine-tuning the instrument of spiritual transformation—that is, *you*. In the first part of this book, we'll explore why. We'll also look at some of the nomenclature and protocol surrounding the practice of traditional monastic psalmody, so that you'll be up to speed the next time you go on retreat.

The fun begins with the "how." In part two of this book, the goal is to help you get up and running in the practice. Even if you can't read music, or if somewhere along the way you've absorbed the message that your voice is no good or you can't sing on key, I still hope to show you that chanting the psalms is accessible to nearly everyone.

Do I really mean this? You bet. You may assume that I'm a talented musician or trained singer—certainly unlike yourself! Hopefully, you'll be disabused of this notion when you listen to the accompanying CD. I'm an amateur musician like most of you. When I sing in choirs, I'm well hidden in the alto section and contribute mostly because I can sight-read a bit and because I've learned how to use my voice in a way that doesn't intrude. I'm no musical genius, that's for sure, and I've never done a solo in my life. But the point I'm making is that no such musical virtuosity is necessary for chanting the psalms. It doesn't take a solo voice, and you don't even need to know how to read music. Starting with simple monotones (singing on one note), I'll show you how to chant any psalm in the Psalter, how to pick up simple psalm notation (either by sight-reading or by ear), and how to find your way around the monastic office well enough to participate meaningfully while on retreat. We'll also look at how to find translations and editions that work for you, how to alter and customize them, and how to chant psalms with your meditation group. This book is primarily a practical handbook, intended to provide everything you need to become fully immersed in the practice of Christian sacred chanting. The accompanying CD contains a basic warm-up exercise for your voice, then musical examples of all the major skills covered in this book.

There's a hidden wisdom in psalmody that makes sense of the practice itself and pulls a lot of the other elements in the Christian contemplative path together. My hope is that, through this book, you'll see what this wisdom is. But even more, that you'll experience it for yourself.

Acknowledgments

LIKE A GOOD WINE, a book such as this is a product of time. My thanks go first and foremost to my two monastic "homes": New Camaldoli Hermitage in Big Sur, California, and St. Benedict's Monastery in Snowmass, Colorado—where for more than two decades I, and all retreatants, have been welcomed into the choir for the daily chanting of the Divine Office. Through the mentorship and hospitality of these monks I was able to learn the art of contemplative psalmody from the inside out.

To Tami Simon and Sarah B. Wheeler at Sounds True, Ltd., in Boulder, Colorado, who first helped me shape this material into an audiocassette teaching series, *Singing the Psalms* (still in print!). To Anne Simpkinson, who imaginatively transposed this series into a regular column at www.Beliefnet.com, and to David O'Neal at Shambhala Publications, who recognized a book here and stood by me graciously and wisely as I expanded and consolidated the material, bringing it into its present form.

To the many monks and others who have read this material on behalf of their communities, offered valuable insights and corrections, and helped with the clearing of musical permissions: Father Micah Schonberger at St. Benedict's Monastery; Fathers Cyprian Consiglio, Isaiah Teichert, Thomas Matus, and Louis Coddaire of New Camaldoli; Father

Tom Francis at Our Lady of the Holy Spirit, Conyers, Georgia; Prior Brad-ford Wolcott of the Fraternités Monastiques de Jérusalem, Strasbourg; Brother Jean-Marc for the Communauté de Taizé; and Macha Capony for the Abbaye de Sylvanès. A special thanks to Louis Coddaire, who was able to shed light on the early days of vernacular chanting at New Camal-doli, and to modestly confess to "probable authorship" of two of the Camaldolese psalm tones used in this manuscript.

To Father John-Julian of the Order of Julian of Norwich and Sister Cintra Pemberton of the Order of Saint Helena, both of whom gifted me with a copy of their communities' respective chantbooks and provided valuable insights into contemporary Anglican monastic psalmody.

To Maria Malunchuk, for her introductions, helpful translations, and steady support as I worked with the French material. To my dear friend Nan Merrill, who generously made available her wonderful translations in *Psalms for Praying* as libretti for my psalm tones. And to Natalie Gi-boney and Michael Boschert, who helped immeasurably with the clear-ing of permissions.

To the entire staff at Shambhala Publications, who have exerted their legendary skill, taste, and competence on behalf of this book to bring its potential to the finest possible fulfillment.

To Julie Paxton and Scott MacCracken, dear friends and skilled musicians in Aspen, Colorado, who generously donated their time to cre-ate the instructional CD accompanying this book. And to Jamie Rosen-berg of Great Divide Studio for his patience, sensitivity, and skillful engineering.

Finally, and in a special way, I wish to acknowledge the mentorship of three remarkable spiritual maestros, each recently departed this planet, who in a special way have brought this book into being and given it its heart and soul: Father Theophane Boyd of St. Benedict's Monastery (1929–2003), Brother Roger of Taizé (1915–2005), and Father Romuald

Duscher of New Camaldoli (1948–2006). Through the beauty of their mature Christian lives, I have been able to see that the path promised in the chanting of the psalms does in fact bear fruit.

CYNTHIA BOURGEAULT
April 2006

Chanting the Psalms

Introduction

The Hidden Wisdom of Psalmody

THE ALARM GOES OFF AT 3:09, a good three hours before dawn will break over this Colorado mountain valley. I throw on my clothes, drive the mile or so to Saint Benedict's Monastery, and am in my seat in the chapel by 3:29, just under the wire, to join the monks for vigils, their traditional night prayer.

Except for a flickering candle beneath an icon and the backlit stained-glass window on the far wall, the chapel is dark. The monks, in white robes, have gathered silently on benches in the very back of the church. As the hall clock sounds a single chime, Brother Thomas intones the psalm verse, "O Lord, open my lips," and the brothers respond, "And my mouth will declare your praise." Then, to the unison chanting of Psalm 134 ("O come bless the Lord, all you who fear the Lord"), the brothers move into the chapel itself, their white robes occasionally catching the play of light from the candle and window. It is like light emerging and disappearing again into darkness—mysterious, silent.

The service unfolds according to an ancient, unhurried rhythm. There is a psalm, a reading from scripture, silence for three or four minutes. Then another psalm, a reading from a commentary (either ancient or modern), and another period of silence. Then a chanted psalm, a spoken psalm, a reading of the Gospel, and a blessing from the abbot.

Then the monks silently disperse, either to the refectory for a cup of coffee before the hour-long meditation that will begin at 4:30 or to their cells for individual prayer and lectio divina, a meditative reading and reflection on scripture.

For the twelve brothers of Saint Benedict's Monastery and the occasional hardy guests who join them, the nightly participation in vigils carries on an ancient tradition that has been handed down in its present form from the sixth-century Rule of Saint Benedict. In other Benedictine monasteries all over the world, monks are performing the same ritual, rising from their sleep for the "night work" that finds its wellspring in Psalm 130: "My soul longs for the Lord more than the watchmen for the morning." During the day, the monks will gather again at regular intervals to refresh themselves in prayer and psalmody. At Saint Benedict's, this takes place at sunrise, before and just after the midday meal, and in the evening just before bedtime. It's called the Divine Office, the cornerstone of Benedictine monastic life.

For many contemporary people, this monastic fascination with the psalms is intriguing and even uplifting. Nearly everyone who goes on retreat at a monastery gravitates to the chanting of the Divine Office as the high point of their experience. Some speak of a mysterious depth and presence they experience there. Almost all single it out as what makes the monastery feel special, a place apart. Kathleen Norris, in her best-selling book *The Cloister Walk*, waxes eloquent about the time she spent in monastic choir during her year as an ecumenical fellow at Saint John's Abbey in Minnesota.[1] She succeeds as well as anyone I know in explaining why this monastic program actually works, what mysterious transformative power may be lurking beneath the seemingly arcane practice of chanting the psalms.

I certainly know whereof she speaks. During the years I lived beside Saint Benedict's Monastery, I was a vigils junkie. The alarm was permanently set for 3:09, and every night for four years, under starry skies or

gathering blizzards, I made that mile-long drive a⟍
join the monks in their simple but profound night ⟍
on the soul that transcends rational explanation.

But bringing the psalms home is quite a different ⟍
other monastic spiritual practices—contemplative p⟍
mindful work—have proven themselves entirely adapt⟍
the cloister walls, the tradition of sacred psalmody has⟍
difficult to transplant. While the Divine Office may be t⟍
the monastic program of spiritual transformation, it conti⟍
sell among contemporary lay contemplatives. I suspect⟍
major reasons for this, one of them intellectual, the other ⟍

Intellectually, many people are puzzled—and frankly, put off—by the insistence on the psalms as the libretti for chanted prayer. The psalms clearly belong to an Old Testament spiritual milieu, and they are often fraught with violence, self-righteousness, and vindictiveness. There is much black-and-white thinking and demonization of the enemy. The teachings seem on a lower level than the teachings of Jesus. How can steeping oneself so intimately in this primitive material bring one to a higher spiritual level? How does it increase compassion and inclusivity? If anything, would it not be better to chant the teachings of Jesus himself or of enlightened Christian masters such as Saint Francis, Meister Eckhart, Julian of Norwich, or Saint Therese of Lisieux? Surely working with sentiments of nobility and compassion would be more conducive to transformation than this stubborn insistence on the psalms, historical though they may be.

And practically speaking, the prospect of chanting the psalms may at first look like it takes a steep learning curve for perhaps dubious gain. You do not pick up the practice automatically; it requires a certain musical skill (not as much as you might initially fear, as I'll try to show in this book, but it's only honest to acknowledge that the tradition takes a certain amount of work to master). In contrast to most of the other sacred traditions of the chanted psalmody may seem wordy, perhaps annoyingly so. One of my friends, a sincere and tolerant Buddhist, voices his impression as follows: "Most chant traditions use a mantra to carry you into an immediate experience of oneness. The Christian tradition is the mechanical chanting of prayers."

Why this is not so will require a book (this book!) to explain, but considering where my friend is coming from, his point is well taken. If you're used to chanting as a means of awakening the chakras, quieting the mind, and plunging into an experience of oneness, the Christian tradition is likely to strike you as hopelessly mental and cumbersome. The constant flow of language in the psalms keeps the mind and emotions engaged and seems to thwart what is usually considered to be the primary purpose of sacred chanting, to carry one beyond the realm of thought.

Any or all of these reasons may leave you hesitant to actually engage in the practice of chanting the psalms, despite its pride of place in monastic life. You may even find yourself wondering whether this practice is still relevant in our much more cosmopolitan and interspiritually oriented day and age. To put it bluntly, has the classic tradition of Christian sacred chanting become a spiritual white elephant? Although beautiful and moving from a distance, is it too tied to institutional monasticism and too cerebral and musically challenging to be of real service to today's contemplative awakening? Has a fifteen-hundred-year-old tradition reached a dead end? And if so, where does one look for a new beginning?

I am not going to answer these questions for you, but if I do my work well, I will at least lay the groundwork by which can make up your mind. When Saint Benedict set out in the early sixth century to found what he called his "school for the Lord's service," he made the Divine Office the backbone of his curriculum and spelled out, chapter and verse, the order and protocol of the psalmody. Was this simply piety, or did he know something we're overlooking? Was there something in the work with those core elements of chanting—breath, tone, attention—that essentially amounted to an underground yoga, an unspoken science of spiritual transformation? Was it merely coincidental that Gregorian chant grew up around this core yoga, with its consistent uplifting thrust toward the higher chakras? Did the psalmody, in spite of or because of its shadow elements, catalyze a process of emotional purification that was prerequisite for further spiritual growth?

To the best of my knowledge, these questions have never been asked before—and they deserve to be. Because psalmody itself, understood as a system of spiritual transformation, is neither so quaint nor so lacking in self-awareness as many people routinely assume. More is going on beneath the surface than meets the eye. As you begin to appreciate the subtlety of this practice, you may be more willing to brave the inevitable learning curve involved in incorporating chanting the psalms as the cornerstone of your own contemplative life.

To be sure, there are winds of change blowing across the map of Christian spirituality. As contemplative practice continues to leap the walls of the monastery and enter the mainstream of modern secular life, new trends and movements toward simplification of the traditional monastic psalmody and even new forms of chanting much more akin to classic mantric chanting are evident. We'll be looking at some of these new movements in the course of this book. The last word on Christian sacred chanting has by no means been written. One of the most exciting things about the present era is that new currents are coming to life even as I write, and contemplative Christians will have the opportunity to engage and refashion their received tradition with an impact not possible before. The window of opportunity is wide open, and those who are prepared and consistently work with the practice itself will move through it gracefully and with enormous influence on the shape of things to come.

In the final analysis, this is not an either-or proposition. To embrace the new currents stirring in Christian sacred chanting does not require a jettisoning of the old. In fact, as you learn to navigate your way through the practices and protocol of traditional psalmody, you may be surprised to discover that the white elephant is not quite as dead as you first thought. Inscrutable as it may first seem, there is a mysterious vital current that flows between the psalms and Christian inner awakening, each pole reviv-ifying and intensifying the other. This current defies rational description, but it does exist, and you can experience it for yourself as it cuts its chan-nel deeper and deeper into your heart. That experience is what this book is really all about.

 *Part One*

The HIDDEN WISDOM
of PSALMODY

I

The PSALMS
of ANCIENT ISRAEL

F ATHER THEOPHANE, the well-loved choirmaster at Saint Benedict's Monastery, had a ready answer for those who asked him about the monastic tradition's great affection for psalmody: "I like to think that I'm praying in the same words that Christ used."

The point he was driving at is obvious: when it comes to the psalms, we are standing on some of the most ancient holy ground in our common Judeo-Christian heritage. The psalms go back a long, long way—*how* long nobody knows for certain, but at least three thousand years is a safe bet. By the time the young Jesus was learning to sing psalms, he was being formed in a tradition whose headwaters had already disappeared into antiquity. Like Father Theophane, he, too, seemed to find reassurance praying in the words that his forefathers used. Again and again the Gospels depict Jesus as responding to questions about himself and his mission by quoting a verse from the psalms, most dramatically in his last words on the cross: in Matthew, Mark, and Luke, "My God, my God, why have you abandoned me?" (Psalm 22:1); and in John, "Father, into your hands I commend my spirit" (Psalm 31:5). They seem to have formed the basic vessel for his self-understanding.[1]

You'll often hear them called the "psalms of David," and indeed, a number of the psalms have traditionally been ascribed to King David, Israel's celebrated warrior-king who captured Jerusalem around 1000 B.C.E. and ushered in the golden era of Israel's fame and glory. Much like the later ascription of Gregorian chant to Pope Gregory, this tradition almost certainly combines a core of truth and a good deal of legend. But the image of the musical King David with his harp and his poetry is vividly imprinted on Biblical tradition, and the psalms are certainly steeped in his spirit, even though we can't pinpoint his actual ownership.

As the psalms came to be written down (in the Old Testament of the Christian Bible and in the Writings, or third division, of the Hebrew Old Testament), they take form as 150 sacred poems—or "songs," to be more specific, since that's what the word *psalm* means.[2] Some psalms are very short—only two or three verses—while others go on for dozens or even hundreds of verses. Biblical scholars generally group them in five major categories according to genre: hymns, laments, songs of thanksgiving and confidence, royal psalms (which are ceremonial in nature), and didactic or teaching psalms.

Despite the pervasive memory of King David, it's very difficult to assign even an approximate dating to most of the psalms. Reputable scholars have been known to vary in their estimate of a given psalm by as much as a thousand years (Psalm 68, for example, has been assigned both to the period of the Judges, which predates King David by more than a century, and to the time of the Maccabees, meaning the second century B.C.E.). Taken individually, it's very difficult to pin down any given psalm within even a range of several centuries, although fortunately, a few psalms that refer to specific historical events can be dated somewhat more precisely.[3]

But perhaps individual dating is the wrong focus of attention, for the psalms are really a seamless whole, rather like a tapestry. Whenever and wherever an individual thread may have originated is far less important

than the total impact of the design. As a whole, the psalms are both coherent and unified in their impression. Situated as they are within the
Wisdom writings of the Old Testament, they offer a haunting, lyrical
counterpoint to the historical narrative itself. Here you'll find recounted
and reworked the essential drama of the story of Israel: the escape from
captivity in Egypt and triumphant entry into the Promised Land; the glory
days of King David and King Solomon, when Israel's fortunes reached
their pinnacle; the slow slide from glory amid gathering inner doubt and
outer embattledness; the destruction of Jerusalem; the exile in Babylon;
the miracle of the restoration, and the slow maturation of this miracle into
a firm messianic hope. All of this is the sacred ground trodden and retrod-
den in the psalms, as these unknown singers pondered the meaning and
personal implication of those mighty events known collectively as "salvation history." The psalms have been called "a microcosm of the whole Old
Testament," "the grand themes of the Old Testament recapitulated under
the form of prayer."[4] They arose from the heart and soul of the people of
ancient Israel to give voice to Israel's unique and remarkable sense of spiritual destiny. They are Israel's love song, its collective memory, its hope,
and its passion.

An Adventure in Consciousness

If you read the psalms carefully, you may notice a story unfolding within a
story. Beneath the outer adventure of kingdoms and conquests, losses and
gains, the psalms bear witness to an even more remarkable and universal
inner adventure.

Fascinatingly, the period during which the bulk of the psalms are
thought to have been composed (800–200 B.C.E.)—corresponds exactly
with a time in world history known as the axial period. Universally and apparently spontaneously, human spiritual consciousness seemed to take a
dramatic lunge forward. In China, this was the era of Lao-tze and Confu-

cius, from whom emerged Chinese philosophy. In India, this period gave birth to the sacred writings known as the Upanishads and also to the teachings of the Buddha. In Greece Pythagoras, Socrates, and Plato were laying the foundations of Western philosophy, while in Persia, the mystical teachings of Zoroaster introduced into Near Eastern consciousness the notion of a cosmic struggle of good and evil, as well as the possibility of personal choice and personal salvation. In Israel, this was the era of the great prophets and Wisdom philosophers. The peak of this period, about 500 B.C.E., occurred just after Israel's return from exile in Babylon.

The nature of this consciousness shift can perhaps be summed up most vividly in a saying from the prophet Jeremiah:

> In those days they shall no longer say: "The parents have eaten sour grapes, and the children's teeth are set on edge." But all shall die for their own sins; the teeth of everyone who eats sour grapes will be set on edge. (Jeremiah 31:30–31)

In essence, the axial period marks the transition from a collective identity—that is, identity through membership in a tribe—to the emergent consciousness of an individual destiny and an individual accountability. It is a watershed of such momentous importance in the history of civilization that Karl Jaspers, the philosopher who first noted this phenomenon, gave it the name *axial* because, in his estimation, "it gave birth to everything which, since then, man has been able to be."[5] The psalms, which book-end this entire period, are right at the heart of the ferment and capture it brilliantly.

To be sure, the psalms are also well grounded in pre-axial consciousness. Over and over, they sing the song of the collective, the people of Israel, as they journey with their God (Yahweh) who encountered them in the wilderness, led them out of bondage in Israel, and called them into a new relationship based on ethical covenant rather than ritual sacrifice or worship of the gods of nature. This awareness marked a major leap forward in human consciousness—from what philosophers such as Ken Wilber would call "magical consciousness," which is characteristic of primitive people and very young children, to "mythic membership consciousness," the precursor of full, individual awakening.[6] Psalm 115 demonstrates this mythic membership stage quite clearly. In it, you can see a strong sense of relatedness to a God who is beyond nature and idols, but the relationship is carried through the group (the "House of Israel"), not the individual:

> Not to us, Lord, not to us,
> But to your name give the glory,
> For the sake of your love and your truth,
> Lest the heathen say: "Where is their God?"
>
> But our God is in the heavens;
> He does whatever he wills.
> Their idols are silver and gold,
> The work of human hands.
>
> They have mouths but they cannot speak,
> They have eyes but they cannot see;
> They have ears but they cannot hear;
> They have nostrils but they cannot smell.
>
> With their hands they cannot feel;
> With their feet they cannot walk.
> Their makers will come to be like them,
> And so will all who trust in them.
>
> House of Israel, trust in the Lord,
> He is their help and their shield.
> House of Aaron, trust in the Lord;
> He is their help and their shield.

As collective responsibility begins to give way during the axial period to individual relationship and accountability, a whole new element enters the language of religious experience: personal emotion. In this respect, once again, King David may well be the archetypal father of the psalms, for he is clearly the Old Testament's first fully axial character, and the psalms exude the energy of his reckless, no-holds-barred passion for the divine. This emerging personal God can be related to with yearning, joy, devotion, anguish, and heartbreak, with one's most intimate hopes and fears. For the first time, God becomes the Beloved, and the psalms become the love songs.

Listen to some of the new accents that enter the language of the psalms as they bear witness to this evolving journey of human spiritual consciousness. There are heartfelt cries of almost unbearable yearning:

> As the deer longs for running water,
> So my soul longs for you, my God. (Psalm 42)

> My soul waits for the Lord,
> More than the watchman for daybreak . . .
>   (Psalm 130)

Of quiet confidence:

> Like a weaned child in mother's arms
> My soul rests in God. (Psalm 131)

> The Lord is my shepherd; I shall not want.
>   (Psalm 23)

Of terror and desolation:

> Save me, Lord, for the waters have risen up to my
>   neck. (Psalm 69)

My God, my God, why have you abandoned me?
    (Psalm 22)

Do not cast me off in my old age,
Do not desert me when my strength fails.
    (Psalm 71)

Of contrition and self-examination:

I trusted even when I said,
"I am sorely afflicted,"
and when I said in my alarm,
"no one can be trusted." (Psalm 116)

My sacrifice, a contrite spirit,
a humbled, contrite heart you will not spurn.
    (Psalm 51)

Of joy and thanksgiving:

In anguish I cried to the Lord.
He heard me and set me free. (Psalm 118)

I thank you, God, with all my heart,
You have heard the words of my mouth.
In the presence of the angels I will bless you.
I will adore before your holy temple. (Psalm 138)

In fact, according to John Cassian, a fifth-century Christian contemplative master, the power of the psalms is that they carry within them "all the feelings of which human nature is capable."[7]

Nearly three thousand years later, it may be hard to see what's so new about this; it's like trying to look *at* the filter you're looking *through*. The notion of religious experience as first and foremost a matter of personal relationship with God has become such a mainstay of our Western spiritual awareness—and the psalms so much the vessel of this awareness—that it's hard to conceive a time when it was otherwise. But it was. The vision of God as beloved, protector, companion, and shepherd represents a quantum leap in human spiritual consciousness, a whole new language of the journey.

Three thousand years further along this path, of course, our notion of the personal has continued to evolve, and it's important to be aware of our own cultural filters as we approach the psalms, so as not to read into them more than is actually there. The individual expressiveness of the psalms is not the same as the rugged individualism of the nineteenth-century romantic poets, such as Keats or Byron, and believe it or not, the psalms are not primarily private devotional poetry. However personal and intimate the spiritual feelings they express, the psalms remain essentially corporate. They are, above all, the songs of a people, and they came to be written down and preserved in the first place because their primary context was in worship. Think of them as hymns rather than poems. When Jesus is remembered as uttering, "My God, my God, why have you abandoned me?" as his final words, he is not expressing his personal feelings of grief and despair. He is chanting a hymn whose sentiments both match and give larger context to his own experience. The personal nature of the psalms is always in a creative tension with the collective; in later chapters, we will come to see how this is their unique strength as a tool of spiritual transformation.

The Adventure Continues

To look at the psalms as an adventure in human consciousness is in no way to deny their special, intimate connection to the people and memory of Israel. But it sets this memory within a much more universal context, for in a mysterious and dynamic way, the psalms still carry the heart and soul of the ongoing human adventure with God. Earlier in this chapter, I spoke

of the work of Ken Wilber and others who have mapped the levels of consciousness the human family has collectively passed through in its journey
through the ages. These philosophers claim that each of us recapitulates
these same stages in our personal life journey, evolving through magical
and mythic membership consciousness before stepping across that axial
threshold into full individual responsibility before God.

The psalms continue to mirror and guide this passage, both in the
macrocosm and the microcosm. My own suspicion, which I'll attempt to
develop more fully in the course of this book, is that the reason the psalms
have been so well loved in Christian contemplative tradition is not merely
that they allow us to "pray in the same words that Christ used," but that
they offer a vehicle that invites—in fact, compels—the spiritual practitioner to keep working through the "archeological dig" in his or her own
being,[8] using these ancient and timeless words to navigate the difficult
inner terrain in the journey to spiritual maturity. It is this journey that we
will now be considering.

2

EARLY MONASTIC PSALMODY

FATHER THEOPHANE's notion of praying in the words that Jesus used took root early and powerfully in Christian consciousness. As a practicing Jew, Jesus would have lived and breathed the psalms, and the insistence of all four Gospels that the psalms were his own most intimate language of prayer became a strong point of contact for early Christianity.

Contact meant everything to these first-generation Christians. In the aftermath of the resurrection, Christianity's foundational self-awareness was centered in the practice of anamnesis, or sacred remembrance. The Eucharist—then as now the centerpiece of Christian worship—was not a memorial ceremony for a dead master but a mystical reunion with their living master at the celestial banquet; it was they themselves who "passed over" in the sharing of his consecrated body and blood. The early Christians remembered that Jesus had promised to be with them "always, until the end of time," and the method for doing so was through his spirit dwelling in their hearts. If they could see, follow, and obey at this more subtle level, they would remain in a committed fellowship with Jesus, an intimacy not simply to be consummated in the hereafter but to be lived fully in the here and now. They could find their living master by traversing that sacred twelve inches from their heads to their hearts, where a different consciousness lived in them, a living Christ consciousness. Spiritual practice for the early church was supremely a matter of sustaining this living remembrance.

Ironically, it helped during those formative centuries that Christianity was an outlawed religion; to practice it openly was a crime that could lead to martyrdom. The high stakes of declaring oneself a Christian created a powerful intensity of purpose, and the urgent need to be connected with the living master who had triumphed over death put real teeth in the practice of anamnesis.

In the early fourth century, however, Christianity found itself transformed almost overnight from forbidden cult to state religion as the conversion of the emperor Constantine in 313 turned the whole situation end over end. Suddenly Christianity found itself preoccupied with building basilicas, hammering out creeds, creating elaborate liturgical ceremonies, and expressing its newfound sense of "the reign of Christ" through the vestments and trappings of imperial royalty. Some Christians felt that this sudden sweep to religious stardom created an impediment to the full practice of their path. Seeking greater simplicity and purity, they fled into the deserts of Syria and Egypt, first in trickles, then in droves. And they took the psalms along with them.

These spiritual pioneers became known collectively as the Desert Fathers and Mothers. Their ascetic experiments in the name of living remembrance constitute the most powerful and sustained path of inner transformation ever to have arisen in Christianity. Some of these desert contemplatives lived as hermits or in small clusters known as sketes. Others found their way to large monastic complexes where hundreds and even thousands of monks banded together in quasi-military style. But whether solitary or communal, the monks all seemed to root their prayer practice in the words that Jesus used. With the appearance of excellent recent translations by Armand Veilleux, Benedicta Ward, and others,[1] we can begin to have a closer look at these desert spiritual practices, in which we discover (no great surprise) that the basic building blocks are the psalms.

The usual pattern was to recite the psalms (from memory, of course, since both texts and the ability to read them were the exception rather than the rule) interspersed with some simple work such as the plaiting of rope. Depending on the particular form of monastic organization (hermit, skete, or monastery), this solitary psalmody might be augmented by periodic community worship, where the psalms would again be proclaimed as part of the liturgical celebration. There is a strong living memory within later monastic tradition that these early monks recited all 150 psalms in a day. While this may be an exaggeration, it does suggest that the core spiritual practice was a more or less continuous recitation of the psalms during the waking hours. Reciting the psalms was almost as regular as breathing. We know that the manner of this recitation probably involved a form of chanting because of a specific comment made by the desert father Evagrius (345–400): "It is a great thing to pray without distraction, but to chant psalms without distraction is even better."[2]

As Evagrius's comment implies, the psalms formed the core of a basic meditational practice, the tethering of the mind within the words of the psalmody. John Cassian, a fifth-century Desert Father who collected and passed on the desert tradition to the West, recommends the use of a versicle from Psalm 70 as a means of achieving continuous attention in prayer: "O God, Come to my assistance; / O Lord, make haste to help me." Describing this as a practice "that has been handed on to some of us from the oldest of the Fathers," Cassian stresses its efficacy and power: "This short verse is an indomitable wall for all those struggling with the onslaught of demons. It is an inpenetrable breastplate and the sturdiest of shields."[3] Within these earliest monastic traditions, then, the psalms—whether chanted alone or in the assembly—formed the basis not only for celebration and proclamation, but for an entrance into contemplative prayer and the work of inner transformation by focusing the mind within the words of the psalm. They became the chief building blocks through which anamnesis, living memory, was attained and maintained.

The achievement of such inner attention was no easier then than it is now. But throughout the whole of monastic tradition we find an acknowledgment of the difficulty as well as encouragement to persist; in fact, the psalms seem to be the place par excellence where the path of inner attention is slowly and painfully achieved. As Saint Romuald would later counsel, "Take every opportunity to sing the psalms in your heart and understand them in your mind. And if the mind wanders as you read, do not give up; hurry back and apply your mind to the words once more."[4]

A School for the Lord's Service

The era of desert spirituality reached its peak in the West in about the early fifth century. By that time, the desert tradition had already begun to jump the Mediterranean. John Cassian, whom we met in the last section, was the key bridge person handing on this torch of living remembrance from the desert to the Christian West. At small monasteries along the southern coasts of France and Italy, monks began to study, write down, and codify what had come to them originally as oral tradition, the living legacy of the desert. These efforts came to magnificent fruition in the sixth-century Rule of Saint Benedict, which has guided Benedictine monastic identity to this day.

We know relatively little about its author. He was born about 480 in the region of Nursia, northeast of Rome. After formal education and a deep conversion that culminated in three years of solitude, he went on to establish several monasteries in the area around Rome, including the illustrious community of Monte Cassino, where he died toward the middle of the sixth century.

Benedict's spirit really lives in his rule, which—true to the motif of anonymity that pervades his life—is not so much an original composition

as a collection and consolidation of a growing corpus of monastic tradition. In particular, it draws heavily on an earlier (and longer) document,
known as the Rule of the Master. Benedict's original and unique genius
shines through in the way he manages to consolidate this rule and shape
it into a coherent and integrated purpose. Under his guiding hand, the
Rule becomes a spiritual path.[5]

Benedict's "school for the Lord's service," as he termed this path, is
founded on a common life of prayer and work—*ora et labora*, as it's still
known. Building on well-established monastic protocol, he grounded the
prayer part of his template in contemplative psalmody.

With the Rule of Saint Benedict, the Divine Office makes its official
debut. The term *Divine Office* is a loose translation of the Latin phrase
Opus Dei, which means "the Work of God"; in Benedict's vision, the chief
work of God for a monk was to offer prayer and psalmody at regular intervals around the clock. Thirteen of the Rule's seventy-three chapters are
dedicated to elaborating the format of Benedictine liturgical psalmody.

Benedict's monastic day actually gets underway in the middle of the
night with the service (or "office") of vigils, somewhere between two and
three in the morning. In addition to this night prayer, Benedict appoints
seven other offices during the day, taking his cue from Psalm 119:164:
"Seven times a day have I praised you." These are lauds (at sunrise), prime,
terce, sext, none, vespers (at sunset), and compline (just before retiring).
The four "little hours" (the Latin names designate "first hour," "third
hour," "sixth hour," and "ninth hour") roughly correspond to 6 A.M., 9
A.M., noon, and 3 P.M.

The Rule assigns psalms to each of these offices, allowing some flexibility "provided that the full complement of 150 psalms is by all means
carefully maintained each week." Benedict adds that monks who in a
week's time say less than the full Psalter, "betray extreme indolence and
lack of devotion in their service. We read, after all, that our holy fathers,
energetic as they were, did this all in a single day."[6]

In most modern Benedictine monasteries, there is some slippage from this ideal, but the ideal itself remains in place. The little hours are very short services (ten to fifteen minutes in length) using what are known as fixed psalms, which means that the same psalms are always said or sung at every service. Large segments of Psalm 119 are worked through during these little hours, since this massive (176 verses) teaching psalm has traditionally been seen as depicting the perfect monastic role model. The greater hours—vigils, lauds, and vespers—have variable psalms, which means that the psalms change from day to day and week to week.

Vigils, the night office, is by far the longest and most complex, based on three nocturns, or ten- to twenty-minute modules, each consisting of psalmody, sacred reading from the Bible or patristic fathers, and prayer. In contemporary monasteries, the format tends to be pared down somewhat, but the office still takes a good forty minutes; in medieval monasteries, it was not uncommon for vigils to go on for well over an hour. This slow-paced, complex office has traditionally been the place where a lot of ground is covered in catching up to Benedict's ideal of all 150 psalms in regular weekly usage.

Each of the day offices begins with the invocation "O God come to my assistance, O Lord make haste to help me," which you will recall is the versicle from Psalm 70 specified by John Cassian as the "inpenetrable breastplate." Vigils begins with "O Lord, open my lips and my mouth shall proclaim your praise" (Psalm 51:15), a fitting beginning for the monastic day and the lines you will still hear being intoned at Benedictine monasteries today to break the silence of the night. The veins of tradition run rich and deep.

If you've spent time at a Benedictine monastery, you've experienced firsthand the effect of this continuous ambient psalmody; it's the source of the rhythm and spaciousness that most visitors find so profoundly moving. With offices every three hours or so, the Benedictine monastic day unfolds, just as Saint Benedict had envisioned, in a balanced alternation between work and prayer, and the monks' workday is punctuated by these regular "pit stops" of psalmody to help keep living remembrance front and center.

I saw this pattern classically at work a few years ago during a brief stopover at Mount Saviour Monastery in upstate New York. That monastery has as one of its means of livelihood a very large sheep farm. As I went up the driveway amid a peel of bells announcing none, the midafternoon office, I noticed a monk in the sheep barn fully immersed (literally as well as figuratively) in his job of shoveling out the sheep pens. Without missing a beat, he set down his shovel, beelined across to the church, and took his place in the choir, a monastic cowl hastily pulled on over his work clothes and his muddy boots replaced with sandals. From all corners of the monastery, other monks were assembling in the choir stalls. A bell rang, the "O God, come to my assistance" was intoned, and for about ten minutes the monks beautifully sang the psalms and simple prayers of this little office. Then, they dispersed just as quickly as they had arrived. As I drove back out, the sheep barn monk was already back to his shoveling.

You might argue that this is quite inefficient. Why not take all those little ten-minute services, consolidate them into one longer service, and open up a block of time where work can get done without all the interruptions?

That's the contemporary model, of course, and many Benedictine monasteries have yielded to it, particularly those with teaching or other active ministries where monks are away from the monastery during working hours. But something is always lost in this capitulation to the contemporary gods of efficiency and the 24/7 work ethic.

For what Benedict's rule really compels a monk to do is to become "biaxial," as it were, living his or her[7] daily life not only along the horizontal timeline, but along the vertical one as well. The vertical timeline is that anamnesis we spoke about at the beginning of the chapter, the continuing remembrance of the eternal now, the deeper reality in which all linear time is grounded and which is the real point of the monastic vocation.

Most of us are drowning in the horizontal most of the time—and this is as true for monks as it is for those in secular occupations. Our work, our immediate goals, our performance anxiety become so all-consuming that we lose track of the vertical axis. That's what spiritual tradition calls "forgetfulness" or "falling asleep": it means losing yourself in the horizontal. But the Rule of Saint Benedict is intent on at least setting some alarm clocks. The great pedagogical mission of Benedict's school for the Lord's service—theoretically, at least—is to create conscious human beings, aware of themselves in time and space but even more deeply aware of themselves as grounded in being itself: "Not what I am, but *that* I am," in the words of a fourteenth-century English monk, who adds that in this deeper consciousness we are "one with God."[8]

Many times during monastic retreats I've had the opportunity to watch this tug-of-war going on within myself. There was one retreat in particular when I'd come with a major writing deadline facing me the day of my return; unfortunately, this would be a "working retreat." I'd been struggling all afternoon with my final book chapter and was just coming down the home stretch when the bell began ringing to announce vespers.

I wrestled with myself, I'll admit. It would have been easy just to skip it and continue with my writing. But something marched me there, for which I am deeply thankful. I returned to my cell a half hour later and polished off the chapter in about ten minutes. But my whole attitude had shifted. Before, my work had *me*; I could see no further than the goal of accomplishment. When I returned, the writing seemed to roll out of me like water flowing downhill from that larger and more spacious sense of orientation, remembering what I was really here for.

Of course, Benedict was on to that wavelength too. Showing up sullen or half-asleep was not the point of psalmody; inner reorientation was. Reaffirming the desert understanding that psalmody is in essence mindfulness prayer, he writes in the Rule, "Let us consider how we ought to behave in the presence of God and his angels, and let us stand to sing the psalms in such a way that our minds are in harmony with our voices."[9]

A good reminder, as timely now as it was fifteen hundred years ago. And just as difficult.

3

PSALMODY *as* CHRISTIAN YOGA

F OR MORE THAN TWELVE HUNDRED YEARS—from somewhere in the Dark Ages until our own times—the church's tradition of con-templative chanting and psalmody was carried largely through the majes-tic vessel of Gregorian chant. When the monks assembled in their choir stalls seven times a day for the psalms and short prayers appointed for each office, it was in Gregorian chant that they sang. Mysterious and ethereal, it is one of the great artistic and spiritual treasures of the Christian con-templative tradition.

This relatively hidden treasure was suddenly thrust into the public limelight about a decade ago when a CD called *Chant*, recorded at an ob-scure Benedictine monastery in Spain, suddenly made it to the top of the pop charts. For many contemporary North Americans, it was their first clue that Christianity actually had a tradition of sacred chanting, let alone one of such unparalleled beauty and spiritual intensity. As the CD spun its magic, many marveled at what they were hearing and wondered what spir-itual practices or altered states of consciousness could have created such sublimity. But beneath the aura of the exotic that the recording so success-fully conveyed, the monks of Santo Domingo de Silos were simply doing what they had been doing since time immemorial—gathering in the chapel to sing the Divine Office.

Gregorian chant and the Benedictine tradition of contemplative psalmody are not identical, although they have been closely intertwined almost from the start. The name "Gregorian chant" is another of those allusive teasers, like the "psalms of David." The artform is generally believed to have taken its name from Pope Gregory I (540–604), who was born about sixty years after Saint Benedict (in fact, he wrote the only known biography of the saint) and was an ardent patron of the spiritual life, monasteries, and the spiritual arts. Tradition has it that Gregorian chant was developed and codified during his papacy, although exactly what hand he had in this process is hard to say, and recent scholarship has called even the tradition itself into question.[1]

However, to say that Gregory or anyone else "composed" Gregorian chant would technically be an anachronism, because the chant wasn't composed at all—if by *composed* one means created and written down by a single individual or even a committee effort. One of the most amazing things about this rich and complex body of sacred art is that it wasn't written down on a musical score until the tenth century at the very earliest. As still tends to be the case today, chant is "pointed," rather than notated—that is, a series of lines and squiggles above the words being chanted jog the memory as to whether the musical line is going up the scale or down. Continuing the tradition received from the Desert Fathers and Mothers, the art of chanted psalmody involved a good deal of memory rather than reading—"listening with the ear of the heart," as Benedict stipulated in his Rule.

Perhaps the most accurate description of the origin of Gregorian chant is "from above." There is such a thing as objective art, revealing such an extraordinary degree of spiritual intelligence and elegance that it seems to emerge from a consciousness beyond even the highest human genius. Gregorian chant is unquestionably of this order. Its ethereal beauty is merely the reflection in sound of a sacred geometry so precise and compelling that it not only lifts the eye of the heart toward the sacred, but actually raises the level of being of the one who participates in it. In the language of the Christian inner tradition, Gregorian chant is an arcanum, a highly conscious art that not only teaches but transforms.[2]

What has never been observed—at least not in any musicological or monastic treatise I have ever read—is that the Divine Office, sung in Gregorian chant, was never simply about piety, or beauty, or even mystical devotion. In the three to five hours spent daily in the choir, the monks were also submitting themselves to a highly precise system of inner alchemy. Whether consciously articulated this way or not, the chanting was a kind of yoga, producing definite changes in the subtle energetic structure of their being according to a well-calibrated blueprint.

Many people, reading the Rule of Saint Benedict from contemporary spiritual reference points, will ask where the actual spiritual practices reside. Other religious traditions have elaborate training in conscious breathing, meditation, raising the *chi* (life energy) through the chakras, stimulating the inner body through conscious vibration, and strengthening the power of conscious attention. On all these points the Rule is curiously silent. There are long chapters on humility and the correct ordering of outer affairs, a few passages on mindfulness ("Let the monks regard all utensils and goods of the monastery as sacred vessels of the altar, aware that nothing is to be neglected."[3]), and some wise and balanced advice about living together in community. But, some people wonder, where is the heart fire, the actual technology of transformation? My sense is that it's all right there, lurking just below the surface, in the Divine Office. The esoteric training was really accomplished in the choir, with Gregorian chant as the premiere vessel for the actual rearrangement of conscious perception.

I first came to suspect this out of my own personal experience as a performing medieval musician. As part of our training in the University of

Pennsylvania Collegium Musicum we spent one summer of intense immersion in Gregorian chant. It probably goes without saying that this form of chanting is highly demanding musically. Fluid and melismatic, it requires precise control of breath and intonation, a deep listening ear so that the entire choir sounds like a single voice, and the power to energize a musical line by feeding it continuous attention. When we emerged from six hours a day of rehearsal, we were actually high! All of our perceptions were heightened, including most strikingly, the heart perception. The world shimmered with a kind of hypervitalized tenderness.

Interestingly, this personal experience is confirmed in a now classic story told by Alfred Tomatis, the famous French eye and nose specialist.[4] In a monastery in southern France some forty years ago, he was called in for a consultation because the monks had mysteriously fallen ill. Almost every kind of remedy had been tried—medication, diet, more exercise or less exercise, rest—but the malaise still lingered. Finally, searching more deeply for a cause, Tomatis discovered that not long before, the abbot had joined the modern trend of scrapping the Gregorian chant and diminishing the length of time the monks spent in chanting the Divine Office. Tomatis called for the chant to be restored, and almost instantly, the monks started to revive. It turned out that their beautiful Romanesque chapel was actually a perfectly tuned reverberating bowl, allowing the monks to receive energy—actual physical sustenance—directly from the vibrations of the chant. Removing it had left them malnourished.

New Wineskins

Thus, you can understand the horror in some quarters when, in the mid-1960s, in the wake of a great church council known as Vatican II, the Catholic Church shelved its tradition of Gregorian chant in favor of simpler chant forms in the vernacular. Many people, for whom the Church's tradition of contemplative psalmody is inseparable from Gregorian chant, have looked on this as an unmitigated disaster—the loss of the entire tradition. A few churches and monasteries flatly refused to cooperate, and in pockets here and there, you will still find the traditional Latin Mass and Gregorian psalm tones in use. Most of the Church got on board, however, with a mixture of reluctance and hope. Almost overnight the *Liber Usualis* (the great compendium of Gregorian chant tones for the Mass and offices) disappeared from the monastic choir rooms as a brave new era of experimentation and adaptation got under way.

I myself am still very much of two minds about this revolution. From my training as a musician and a student of the Christian inner tradition, I am all too aware of the subtle precision of the chant as a tool of transformation. In its usual bumptious fashion, the Church meddled with and wrecked a conscious art without fully realizing what it was doing, and the consequences stand for themselves. Dr. Tomatis's encounter with those flagging monks in southern France may well have been a poignant herald of things to come, for in many ways contemplative monasticism has yet to recover from the blow. In particular, the Cistercians (Trappists), whose whole monastic program was built on concentrating and intensifying the energy of mystical love, have suffered greatly from the loss of what, unknown even to them, may have been the driveshaft of their transformational turbine.[5]

On the other hand, the transcendent realms always seem to be creating new wineskins for the wine of conscious transformation. It is true that for more than a millennium Christian monasticism and Gregorian chant have been deeply intertwined, but they are not inseparable. After all, Jesus never sang Gregorian chant. Nor did the Desert Fathers and Mothers. The underlying transformative principle has to be deeper. As the thrust of our own spiritual times seems to relentlessly break up the old monastic containers and push the contemplative path out into the world, Gregorian chant is simply not a realistic vehicle to carry forward this new movement of the spirit. It is too arcane, too tied to the life of the monastery,[6] and beyond the skill level of most contemporary seekers. In this intuition, the Second Vatican Council was certainly correct. At no small cost to the finger that points to the moon (to reference an old Zen parable), we are permitted once again to look directly at the moon.

So let's begin again with the underlying fundamentals. The yoga of the choir remains. Gregorian chant developed this yoga in a particularly intense and powerful way, perfectly tailored to the context in which it found itself. But the basic transformative principles underlie all sacred chanting, and once you recognize what they are, you can work with them intentionally in any chant form, including the very simple monosyllabic chant we'll be undertaking shortly.

The Four Elements

It has often struck me that chanting, in any tradition, is fundamentally a deep immersion experience in the creative power of the universe. Because to make music, you must work—in your body, mind, and spirit—with the four holy elements out of which the earth was fashioned and through which all spiritual transformation happens.

The first element is *breath*. Father Theophane used to like to remind people, "Every breath you take is the breath of God." Many of the great world religions picture the earth as being created and sustained by the steady, rhythmic "breathing" of God. Virtually every religious tradition starts you off on a spiritual practice by bringing your attention to the breath and teaching you to breathe consciously and fully.

Gregorian chant, of course, works with breath in a particularly intentional way. Because of its long, flowing melismas, it forces you to adopt a breathing pattern of measured exhalation in which the outbreath is substantially longer than the inbreath. You learn to draw a full, conscious inbreath, then release it with a slow, measured count. This training parallels conscious breath work in other sacred traditions and leads to a hypervitalization of the body as the blood cells are flooded with oxygen. But all sacred chanting, no matter how complex, provides the opportunity to practice conscious breathing. In fact, unless grounded in the breath, no chanting is really sacred; it doesn't reach far enough into your being.

The second element is *tone*, or vibration, the sound you make as you add voice to that breath. Again, our religious traditions all tell us that creation came into existence through the power of vibration. The Christian language for expressing this idea is "In the beginning was the Word . . ." (for what else is a word if not vibration?). Mythologically, the world was "spoken" into existence. So when we make a tone, we are participating in the sacred creative act that shapes and sustains all being.

Singers very quickly learn that the only way to make an authentic tone is to start from the center—that place deep inside you, called the diaphragm, where both your breath and the bottom of your vocal column are anchored. Whether a tone is natural and resonant or forced, shrill, and breathy depends on whether you sing from this place. To make an authentic tone, you have to come back to center.

There are a lot of gimmicks to fake or force a tone. But to sing authentically, we have to begin with what we are, not what we're not. When we work with tone in music, we are really working with the deepest and most revealing aspects of our selfhood. Just as you can't fake your true self, you also can't fake your true singing voice. Herein lies one of the greatest transformative powers of the yoga of choir: it catapults you directly into the heart of your own deep selfhood, the authentic ground of all spiritual work.

The third sacred element is *intentionality*, or the meaning of the words. This aspect is particularly important in Christian psalmody. Certainly Christian chant makes use of breath and vibration, as all chant does. But it is not primarily about sacred vibration or about the rhythmic, almost hypnotic repetition of a single phrase or mantra—not traditionally anyway.[7] In Christian sacred chanting, you have to know and understand the words; you have to accept them into your being in a fundamental way. In fact, that's why the Vatican II council instructed that the psalms be translated into the vernacular—English, French, Swahili, and all the languages in which people worship. The meaning of the words is always primary in Christian chanting. Contemplative psalmody is a matter of staying close to the text, of being with it and in it.

It isn't easy, of course, to stay present without the mind wandering—it never has been. Remember that admonition of Evagrius, back in the fourth century: "To chant the psalms is a good thing; to chant the psalms without distraction is an even better thing." In the eleventh century, Saint Romuald added words of encouragement; if the mind wanders, one must gently but firmly keep bringing it back to the psalm. The idea of conscious attention and consent to the meaning of a passage is a key element in the Christian transformational path.

This awareness has immediate repercussions in the choir. The psalms embrace a wide range of emotions, and while you don't have to become emotional yourself, you do have to pay respectful attention to what the words are saying. If you're bored or your head is out to lunch, everything goes wrong in psalm singing: the pitch goes flat, you fall asleep, and the music is dead. Feeding intentionality into your chanting is perhaps the single most important way of making the music—and yourself—stay awake. When you energize the psalm by paying attention, you energize yourself as well, and your singing helps you gain spiritual force rather than losing it.

The fourth sacred element is *community*. A good part of the discipline of the monastic choir—or any choir—lies in the art of listening to one another and adjusting to one another. Everyone sings with a slightly different vocal instrument, and the beauty comes in blending them together through a subtle give-and-take. You also have to be aware of the space that the person next to you is taking up and avoid the temptation to wander off into a personal emotional high. I remember one evening at vespers with the monks at Saint Benedict's when I was so pleased that I knew a particular psalm tone well that I started singing with wonderful drama and verve, having myself a grand old time. Afterward one of the monks pulled me aside and said very sweetly but pointedly, "My choirmaster once told me, if you can't hear the person next to you, you're singing too loud."

Breath, tone, intentionality, and community: it seems like there are a lot of things to pay attention to all at once. But sometimes it all comes together. One Saturday night at Saint Benedict's, when we again gathered for vespers, I looked around to see only a skeleton crew of monks; most of the best singers were away for the evening. "We're in trouble," I thought, for Saturday is the one night of the week when the monks sing the *Salve Regina*, an extraordinarily beautiful and demanding Gregorian hymn in honor of the Virgin Mary which soars to the stratosphere and lasts for more than five minutes.

It took only two seconds for me to realize that we weren't in trouble after all. I have never in my life heard Gregorian chant sung more beautifully. Something in those men kicked in, and the eight of them were singing with one voice, as if one angel was soaring above them, weaving their hearts and souls into a brilliant, utterly moving love song. It was definitely a case of the whole being greater than the sum of the parts. It happened that night because the monks were intensely alive, connected with themselves, each other, and the prayer they were singing. Breath, vibration, emotional intentionality, and community—the heart of the Christian yoga in a laserlike moment of perfection.

It is probably not coincidental that the monks were singing Gregorian chant that evening. As I said earlier, there is a particularly intense chemistry between Gregorian chant and the love mysticism at the heart of the Cistercian charism, and when that chemistry is "on," it attains an unparalleled sublimity. But I have experienced much the same perfection in a very different setting; in fact, it remains one of my most remarkable experiences of sacred chanting. I was coordinating an interfaith worship service in Vancouver, British Columbia, in the spring of 2004, celebrating the visit of the Dalai Lama. As each of seven religious traditions (Hindu, Jewish, Sikh, Christian, Buddhist, Islamic, and Native American) led us in ten minutes of their respective sacred prayers and chanting, the energy in the room began to build.

The plan had called for the service to end with a silent candlelit recessional. But as participants slowly and somewhat reluctantly began to file out, it seemed that something different was being called for, and without fully knowing what I was doing, I launched the chant "Holy, Holy, Holy One." This is a very simple three-part round (to the tune of the old folksong "Hey, Ho, Nobody Home") that our contemplative prayer groups in British Columbia had been working with as part of an ongoing project to develop simple forms of Christian mantric chanting suitable for use with Centering Prayer (I'll speak more about this project in part three of this book).

The chant caught. In an instant, it swept like a grassfire through the crowd, and as the cavernous old church emptied row by row, the singing continued to build. An hour later, when the last row finally exited the building, I emerged into the night to a sight I will never forget. The entire group was still there, gathered in a circle on the sidewalk, and the chant was still going strong. By the light of hundreds of flickering candles, I watched Sufi dervishes whirling beneath Buddhist prayer flags, while Native Americans in feathered headdresses kept the drumbeat, and saffron robes, white turbans, and yamulkes all pressed closely together singing, "Holy, holy, holy one . . ." What a portrait of the human family!

The pictures of those two very different chanting experiences stand closely together in my heart; I don't easily think of either separately. The taste of oneness was the same—the first within a small, cloistered group of men for whom the Gregorian love song to Mary carried infinite yearning and infinite particularity; the second within a far-flung group of human beings, held together by what is most simple and universal in all human experience—breath, tone, intentionality, and community. Somehow these two interlocking vignettes renew my hope that it's not a question of either-or but of both-and. The Christian tradition of sacred chanting has been carried in some magnificent wineskins, but it works in very simple ones too, once they are put in the service of what seems to be the overwhelming movement of the Spirit in our own times: to unite the hearts of all human beings in a mutual compassion that makes a strength of our diversity and creates safety and healing for our planet.

As we begin again with what is most basic and universal in the art of sacred chanting, I am guided by the image of the fruit tree that must be pruned regularly if it is to continue bearing fruit. The Christian tradition has recently come through just such a pruning. In the next part of this book, I hope to show how we are beginning to reap the fruit.

4

The PSALMS *as* PSYCHOLOGICAL TOOLS

B EFORE WE EMBARK on actually chanting the psalms, there is one important issue that we need to confront head-on—namely, whether
we ought to be working with them at all! In point of fact, many contemporary spiritual seekers are reluctant to have anything to do with the
psalms because of their undeniable violence, exclusivity, and patriarchal
language. In the light of our present world situation, can a person in good
conscience really bring himself or herself to pray a prayer such as "destroy
all those who oppress me" (Psalm 143), or even worse, those notorious
lines from Psalm 137:

> O Daughter of Babylon doomed to destruction,
> happy the one who pays you back
> for what you have done to us.

> Happy shall he be who takes your little ones
> and dashes them against the rock!

Sentiments such as these have caused many Christians to conclude regretfully that the psalms are part of the problem, not part of the solution. Isn't this kind of thinking exactly what spiritual practice is calling us to transcend?

To add a bit of perspective, this issue is a very, very old one on the Christian mind map. Way back in the second century, a teacher named Marcion advanced a virtually identical hypothesis: that the God of love revealed so fully in Jesus Christ was incompatible with the warlike and ex-clusivist God of the Old Testament, and Christians should therefore have no further dealings with the Old Testament. This position was judged a heresy (Christianity's first), as the church fathers affirmed that the two tes-taments were inextricably linked, a position the church has held ever since. But as the consequences of this kind of dualistic, violent thinking continue to play themselves out, particularly in the Middle East, Marcion's position comes up for periodic review. I know many Christians, including monks and even abbots long experienced on the path, who have reluctantly concluded that the psalms are a luxury humankind can no longer afford.

My intention in this chapter is not to try to persuade you one way or the other, but to try to address this concern from a wider perspective. Be-fore any decision can be made as to whether the psalms are an appropri-ate vehicle for contemporary spiritual consciousness, it is first necessary to understand more fully the process that is actually set in motion when they are prayed on a regular and sustained basis. The findings may sur-prise you!

Public versus Contemplative Psalmody

Before delving into this conundrum, it's necessary to set the stage by dis-tinguishing clearly between the two traditional uses of psalmody in Chris-tian worship: public proclamation and contemplative prayer. Very different rules and conventions apply to each use.

In proclamation mode, the psalms are recited in church as part of the public worship service—a tradition, as we have seen, whose roots go all the way back to ancient Israel. In today's mainstream liturgical churches (Roman Catholic, Episcopal, Lutheran), the psalms occupy a fixed position in the Eucharistic liturgy between the Old Testament reading and the epistle and are frequently chanted by either the choir or the whole congregation.

In this prominent, public position, I believe there is little excuse for parading forth the darkest and most violent passages in the psalms. It is inappropriate, even flat-out abusive, to indulge in the gratuitous violence of, say, that verse from Psalm 137 in a congregation where little ones are present or to engage the congregation in long diatribes from the "cursing psalms," particularly if there will be no follow-up in the sermon. One has to be mindful, particularly in today's church, that many people sitting in the pews will be hearing scripture "cold," with no previous background and a very literal understanding. The paramount concern must be with congruency and clear communication of the gospel of redemptive love, and this sometimes necessitates a bit of judicious pruning. Saint Paul's advice is germane here: "Let us try never to put in the way of our brother anything that would make him stumble and fall" (Romans 14:14).

But contemplative psalmody is a different ballpark. Here, the starting assumptions are that the psalms are being prayed within the context of some overarching methodology, or school of transformation, and that all 150 will be used with some regularity. This set of conditions creates some very different possibilities and protocol.

Kathleen Norris describes this second playing field well in her book, *The Cloister Walk*, an account of the year she lived in close proximity with the monks of Saint John's Benedictine Abbey in Collegeville, Minnesota.[1] (I have mentioned this book already in the introduction.) Through her participation in the Daily Office, she was thrown off the diving board into the pool of contemplative psalmody, and her fresh insights

ring with deep truth. Her chapter on Benedictine psalmody is not only
one of the strongest in the book, but it is also one of the best cases I have
seen for continuing to honor and make creative use of that shadow material so prominent within the psalms.

Norris observes that the psalms make it okay to talk about pain. Acknowledging not only the bright and uplifting moments on the spiritual
journey but also the dark and awkward, the psalms are a touchstone for
honesty, for getting *real* in one's spirituality. She writes:

> The value of this great songbook of the Bible lies not in the fact
> that singing praise can alleviate pain but that the painful im-
> ages we find there are essential for praise, for without them,
> praise is meaningless. It becomes the "dreadful cheer" that
> Minnesota author Carol Bly has complained of in generic
> American Christianity, which blinds itself to pain and there-
> fore makes a mockery of its praise.[2]

She further observes that "in expressing all the complexities and con-
tradictions of human experience the psalms act as good psychologists.
They defeat our tendency to be holy without being human first."[3] By some
mysterious alchemy, "the daily praying of the psalms helps monastic people to live with them in a balanced and realistic way"[4]—even those passages filled with shadows and violence—and to live with themselves in the
same fashion.

Norris speaks from the perspective of a writer and literary scholar, but
in these several insights, she comes very close to articulating the hidden
wisdom of contemplative psalmody far better than most theological and
ascetical treatises I have read. She rightly intuits that the psalms are in
some sense psychological tools, functioning within the contemplative
milieu primarily as vessels of interior work, whose ultimate goal is to
produce a mature and tempered human being. In the next few pages, I

would like to build on her insights and look at how this alchemy actually happens.

The Unloading of the Unconscious

If you begin a contemplative practice, you *will* encounter the shadow. It is inevitable, for deep contemplative prayer brings us face-to-face with parts of ourselves that we would perhaps prefer not to acknowledge. ·

One of the great breakthroughs in our understanding of the art of contemplative prayer came in our own time when Father Thomas Keating, principal architect of the method of Centering Prayer, recognized that when people meditate for long periods of time—whether by Centering Prayer or some other method—they sooner or later hit some patches of rough sea that he calls "the unloading of the unconscious."[5] As meditation relaxes the inhibitory effect of our usual egoic consciousness, buried memories, pain, and undigested emotional and physical trauma can and do begin to surface.

Keating teaches that this unloading is both normal and profoundly healing—in fact, he calls it "the divine therapy"—for the unrecognized and unintegrated shadow material is precisely the part that keeps tripping us up in our life journey. In Centering Prayer intensive retreats, trained staff are constantly available so that as participants begin this unloading, the material can come up in a safe place, be processed, held as precious, embraced, and released.

In the classic contemplative tradition, I believe this is exactly the role played by psalmody.

You will recall how the psalms were already being depicted by John Cassian in the fifth century as "carrying all the feelings of which human nature is capable." In their various moods and amazingly shrewd insights into the human condition, they really do seem to contain the entire gamut of human emotional experience, from the heights of exaltation to the depths of desolation. And in a week of chanting the Psalter in its entirety, you will run through that full gamut.

Two psalms sung back-to-back at Saint Benedict's Monastery in Colorado on successive mornings make this point only too well. On Tuesdays, lauds included "I said in my good fortune that nothing could ever disturb me" (Psalm 30); on Wednesdays, there was "I said in my alarm, no one can be trusted" (Psalm 116). These two psalms reflect diametrically opposite places in life; I'll bet you'll recognize them both.

Consider the deep spiritual yearning expressed in Psalm 63: "Oh God, for you my soul is thirsting, my flesh is longing / like a dry, weary land without water." Or the deep agony of the cry in Psalm 43: "For you are the God of my strength; / why have you put me from you?" Or the vindictive fury of Psalm 140 as the psalmist rails against his foes: "Let hot burning coals fall upon them; / let them be cast in the mire, never to rise up again." Or the exaltation of Psalm 96: "Sing to the Lord a new song; / sing to the Lord, all the whole earth." Or the quiet calm of Psalm 131: "Lord, I keep my soul at peace, like a weaned child on its mother's breast." Or the deep trustfulness of Psalm 31: "Into your hands I commend my spirit, / for you have redeemed me, O Lord, O God of truth." Like a vast cornucopia of personal experience, the psalms overflow with all the joy, despair, agony, and hope of which we human beings are capable.

What I believe happens when we introduce the psalms into our consciousness—and even more so into our *unconscious*—through the practice of contemplative psalmody is that they begin to create a safe spiritual container for recognizing and processing those dark shadows within ourselves, those places we'd prefer not to think about. There are times in the spiritual journey when anger is a very real part of our life, just as jealousy, abandonment, helplessness, rage, and terror are. All of these emotions are in us, and they're all in the psalms. Perhaps we're not terribly pleased with ourselves when we find ourselves praying, "Destroy all those who oppress me, O Lord," but most of us have felt that way.

Acknowledging the shadow is only part of the healing process, albeit an important part. The other and even more important part is letting it go. This is a place where standard psychotherapy often bogs down. It's not that difficult to raise the issues, to become more conscious of your wounds and neurotic defenses. But without some means of releasing this shadow material, it's all too easy to get stuck in it and even possessive of it; your woundedness becomes a kind of identity badge. Contemplative psalmody provides a graceful way of moving on.

To begin with, while the psalms are intensely personal, they are never simply all about *you*. Remember how I said back in chapter 1 that their emotion is collective more than individual? They belong to the great stream of humanity, and their very antiquity is part of their power. They acknowledge and validate your own emotional reality, but through the mirror of nearly three thousand years of common human experience. "Others have felt this way," they remind you. "Others have passed through these dark places and experienced what you are now experiencing." The psalms offer themselves as transpersonal containers, allowing us to acknowledge our feelings fully without getting stuck in them. And because they belong to the liturgy, the great language of worship and prayer, they also serve as a kind of confessional, allowing us to place our shadow side on the altar of prayer and find our release there.

The process went on even for Jesus. Remember how in those last harrowing moments on the cross he cried out, "My God, my God, why have you forsaken me?" Those words spoken in his agony are from Psalm 22, which in the rabbinical tradition (which Jesus would have known) was the psalm sung at the hour of death. From the depths of his own suffering, he intuitively found his way to this psalm with the last breath of his life.

As you chant the psalms as part of a daily spiritual practice, you are actually preparing a place deep within yourself, a spiritual sanctuary wherein you can acknowledge and pass through violent inner emotions unscathed. You begin to see and trust that what emerges from your unconscious during those times of "unloading" and shadow work is not overwhelming or isolating because others have walked this way before, and prayer upholds you as it did them. Both pain and shame take on a more universal context as you allow yourself to receive help, not only from the psalms themselves, but from the spiritual reality to which they bear unflinching witness. Because staying present to those emotions, even the dark and shadowy ones, is a way of lifting up before God all that you are, your personal woundedness can become the very marrow of your prayer.

The other important aspect of this transpersonal purification is that the Divine Office goes its way with serene indifference to the ups and downs of your own personal psychodrama. You can enter the choir all merry and upbeat from a good day only to be faced with "Even my best friend has abandoned me; my only companion is darkness." Or you can arrive down and despondent and find yourself singing, "The heavens proclaim the greatness of the Lord," or "You have changed my mourning into dancing." The kaleidescopic emotionality of the psalms unfolds as it will, without any regard to where *you* happen to be in your own emotional kaleidescope that day. In and of itself, this process eventually tends to build in a certain detachment from the emotional hurly-burly of your life. You begin to see that all emotions are ultimately just energy events in time and will come and go of their own accord if you don't strain too much to hold on to them. That in itself may be the most important lesson you will ever learn for moving beyond the narcissistically personal into the deeper waters of transformed life.

Thus, contemplative psalmody is a powerful tool for acknowledging the emotions, but an even more powerful tool for releasing, for learning to detach from the surface of yourself and enter into the deeper places of the heart. Kathleen Norris expresses this idea beautifully when she says, "In the dynamic of this liturgy one rides the psalms like a river current . . . I felt as if I were becoming part of a living, lived-in poem."[6]

The Tempering of Being

As long as there is in human nature one dark corner of violence, one dark corner of jealousy, one dark corner of loneliness or abandonment, the psalms will be familiar and relevant. In fact, some of the most profoundly transformed Christians I know have spent a lifetime struggling with the psalms, working through them, and through this work of prayer confronting their own inner darkness at deeper and deeper levels.

I remember a very interesting conversation I once had with a wise elderly contemplative about that line in Psalm 143: "Destroy all those who oppress me, for you are my redeemer, O Lord."

"How can I pray these words and still call myself a Christian?" I asked her.

Without batting an eye, she replied, "This used to bother me too. But what I've come to understand is that this prayer really means destroy in *me* that dualizing tendency of the mind that divides my world up into friends and enemies. Let me see through the eyes of divine Oneness that my so-called oppressors are all projections of my own deepest fears."

She looked at me and twinkled. For sixty years of monastic life, this woman had been taking into her heart the deepest Christian truths of forgiveness and love and laying them unflinchingly alongside her own darkest places. The fruits of this process were plain to see.

Helen Luke, another stellar wisewoman (she died in 1995 at the age of ninety-four) once wrote: "Wholeness emerges out of the acceptance of the conflict between the divine and the human in the individual psyche."[7] There's profound truth to her observation. She realizes that as human beings we live in creative tension with ourselves. There is a divine striving in each of us that "yearns for the courts of the Lord" (in the words of Psalm

84). There is also a human being, shadow and all—not just a cleaned-up and edited version—who longs to come into being. The genuine integration of these two yearnings is the crucible of our own wholeness, and the psalms hold our feet to the fire.

In their deep, earthy honesty, the psalms help us to stay grounded in our own being so that our spiritual practice doesn't become an escape from the psychological work that must be done. This is another reason why intentionality is so important in chanted psalmody. We do not use the psalms to escape into beautiful aesthetic or mystical experiences. Rather, we stand there in our woundedness and authenticity and allow the work of purification and healing to unfold within us through our conscious participation and confession.

And unfold it does. In the next chapter, I will add some nuances to what I am about to say here, but for now it will suffice to return to another keen insight from Kathleen Norris: "The psalms are always instructing the heart."[8] In a language all their own, both concrete and powerfully archetypal, they speak directly to the heart, guiding its progress through the dark patches of the unconscious in its journey toward balance and wholeness. That is why contemporary revisionist criticism that finds fault with the violence of the imagery is misplaced in contemplative psalmody. The psalms are psychological tools. They describe the interior warfare, the desolation, the shadow, and its transfiguration. When you actually take up the practice of chanting the psalms, this will all become very clear to you.

So should we clean them up or not? Kathleen Norris contributes the following vignette: "In recent years, some Benedictine houses, particularly women's communities, have been censoring the harshest of the psalms, often called the 'cursing psalms,' from their public worship. But one sister, a liturgist, said after visiting such a community, 'I begin to get antsy, feeling *something is not right*. The human experience is violence, and psalms reflect the violence of the world.'"[9]

Perhaps this is so. But if the wisdom of contemplative psalmody is fully understood, one could take this observation a large step further and suggest that the psalms, processed in the contemplative heart, *transform* the violence of the world. That, at any rate, has been my own deepest experience of this sacred tradition.

5

The PSALMS *as*
SOUL MUSIC

U NLIKE MOST OF THE GREAT WORLD TRADITIONS of sacred
chanting, which rely on the rhythmic, almost hypnotic repetition
of a single prayer phrase or mantra, Christian psalmody is fast paced and
mentally demanding. Rather than stilling the mind, psalmody floods it
with images and emotions and requires a compassionate engagement
with the meaning of the words themselves. The immediate experience
may be that the chanting feels less ecstatic, more "mental," than in other
sacred traditions. So it may come as a surprise when I say that contemplative psalmody is actually a total immersion program in learning to think
with the heart.

Yes, images and emotions go swirling through you. Contemplative
psalmody operates at the level of the archetypal imagination. While we
saw in the last chapter that some of this work has to do with the integration of the shadow and the healing of the personal unconscious, the real
power of the psalms lies in their uncanny ability to awaken the unitive
imagination.

Unitive imagination means the ability to think with more than just the
linear mind, to engage those faculties of intuition, sensitivity, creativity,

and conscience that lie deep within the psyche and support a "wisdom" way of knowing. Another way of describing this full-spectrum thinking would be "thinking with the heart."

Like all the Western religions, Christianity is a religion of the Word. But that Word is a unitive Word; a heart word. It does not yield itself up easily to a linear, or cause-and-effect, way of thinking. At the literal level, elements in the tradition such as the Virgin Birth or the mystical body of Christ may make no sense at all. But to the awakened unitive imagination, they become precise road maps of the path of inner transformation, increasingly verifiable as those depths of inner silence and recollection increase.

In fact, for much of early Christian tradition, this movement beyond the literal was the whole goal of the spiritual journey. To awaken meant to awaken to an increasingly subtle recognition of the hidden power contained in the language and imagery of scripture, a power capable of sustaining both spiritual and moral illumination. Monks diligently applied themselves to their lectio divina, or sacred reading of the words of scripture, confident that as their hearts were purified through prayer, moral vigilance, and ascetic practices, they would become more and more capable of understanding the sublime truth preserved like finest wine within the sturdy casks of the sacred writings.[1]

The Four Senses of Scripture

According to monastic tradition, this deepening understanding unfolds in four stages, commonly known as the four senses of scripture. They are the milestones on the journey to unitive understanding. While the various monastic orders diverge in their nomenclature for the two middle stages, the basic scenario is the same.[2]

The first stage, the *literal*, is all about facts and linear causality. Did the Virgin Birth really happen? Does Jesus really intend me to cut off my hand or pluck out my eye if it leads me into sin? At this level, the Bible tends to be interpreted as a rule book for daily living, and there is little tolerance for ambiguity.

The literal level gradually gives way to the second phase, called the *christological*. At this point, we begin to see all the stories and images in the Bible as pointing directly to the Christ mystery. Jerusalem, for example, is no longer just an earthly city; it is preeminently a symbol for the church, "the bridegroom of Christ." The Old Testament images of the suffering servant and Son of man are seen as direct foreshadowings of Christ, and Abraham's sacrifice of Isaac in the book of Genesis is a prefiguring of Jesus on the cross.

While this process may seem forced—and if you're not a Christian, even offensive—the *how* of it is actually quite interesting. We are leaving linear causality behind and beginning to see analogically in terms of coincidences, symbols, and resonances—in other words, through the eyes of poetry. Around the center point of Christ, we learn how to tap into the more subtle image-forming and symbolic capacities of an awakening heart.

At the third stage of development, called the *tropological* (which means having to do with growth), we leave behind the Christ mystery as the template through which all emotions must be processed and allow the images to form their own patterns and cross weavings. At this stage, the light begins to dawn that the Bible stories are holograms of the soul's journey. They are rich portraits, in analogical language, of the stages and steps we all go through in the journey of transformation. Jonah and the whale, for example, is no longer discounted simply as a myth or folktale; we see that every new beginning involves a fleeing, a constriction, a darkness, and then being "coughed up" onto new ground. Mary and Martha, the sisters in Luke's Gospel who invite Jesus to dine with them, are no longer two different individuals, but a parable about the Mary and Martha in each of us and how the busy, self-important egoic self must give way to the heart, which knows how to sit in rapt adoration at the foot of the master. Once we begin to hear scripture, it's like suddenly beginning to crack the soul code.

My teacher, Thomas Keating, vividly describes this stage in his own monastic journey, when his novice master assigned him the Old Testament book of Exodus for his lenten scriptural reading. Having hoped to spend Lent with the Gospel of John, he embarked on this task with a heavy heart. But soon his excitement grew as he realized, "This book is talking about my life. Whoever wrote this book must have been my psychiatrist!"[3] He could see how the narrative of the Israelites' escape from slavery in Egypt and miraculous deliverance at the Red Sea was a vivid metaphor for his own conversion experience.

There is still a fourth and subtle stage that is the full emergence of the unitive. At this level of understanding, we become not only sensitive interpreters of the patterns but actually cocreators. The fifth-century Desert Father John Cassian once said he knew his monks had achieved this unitive stage when "they sang the psalms as if they were composing them."[4] If, at the preceding stage, the scriptural story is "all about me," at this last and most sublime stage, we begin to realize that there is only one story, the great Biblical drama of salvation, and our own life is perfectly mirrored and contained within it.

Metaphorical Living

While Saint Benedict may not have had terms such as *archetypal unconscious* and *unitive awakening* at his disposal back in the sixth century, his intuitions in this regard were very keen. His school for the Lord's service was, in essence, a systematic method for the awakening of the unitive imagination. And the core of his curriculum, both qualitatively and quantitatively, was psalmody.

The other parts of the monastic day—manual work together and time alone for study and lectio divina—were arranged around the great trunk root of the Divine Office. As we've seen, this rhythm sets up a dynamic tension between the words of scripture deeply and prayerfully ingested and the circumstances of daily life. Gradually, in this creative tension between being and doing, the monk's life and the living Word of scripture would become more and more intermeshed, until finally they merged completely in the monk's awakened heart.

During the seven years I lived alongside the monks of Saint Benedict's Monastery in Snowmass, Colorado, I had many opportunities to experience the subtle genius of this monastic art form. One dismal, snowy evening in early December, I was down at the pump house struggling to replace a broken hose that had shut off the water up at my house. I'd had three or four tries, icy water up to my knees and on my hands, trying to prime the old pump. At last, it took; the pump hummed to life and the pressure gauge started climbing. Suddenly out of nowhere, I found myself singing a little antiphon from one of those dark early-morning services: "With joy you shall draw water from the fountain of salvation." There I was, muddy and frozen, but suddenly my struggle with the pump briefly found itself in a larger context, and my laughter was for more than just a day's work well done. For a brief moment, I belonged to a story greater than my own.

Monks, in fact, don't speak so much of "hearing" scripture as they do of "ingesting it." Deep in the night, then seven times during the day, the words and images of the psalms are insinuated into their being—not long texts that would stimulate conceptual thinking, but little phrases and images: "As the deer longs for running water, so my soul thirsts for you, O Lord" (Psalm 42); "O Lord, open my lips and my mouth will declare your praise (Psalm 51); "My soul longs for the Lord more than watchmen long for daybreak" (Psalm 130). Bypassing the conscious mind, these lines fall directly into the unconcious, anchored and reinforced by interior prayer and silence. It is almost like an intravenous drip of psalmody, a steady infusion of these ancient images and petitions into the waiting heart.

The music greatly heightens this effect. As anyone who has ever sung in a choir knows, the melodies carry the words down to a level where they are always retrievable, unlike passages simply committed to verbal memory. You will be able to recall the words of something if you remember the tune to which they're set; the key phrases will bubble up out of the unconscious along with the tune, then the rest of the words will gradually fill in.

What happens when the Divine Office becomes the backbone of daily life? Outwardly, a situation such as the poet Charles Baudelaire vividly describes in his poem "Correspondances" is set up—a dynamic tension or dialogue between inner world and outer world carried in the power of images.[5] The events of the day and the ingested bits of psalm verses reach out and connect, as happened to me in the pump house. It was no longer just a grim, miserable job on an equally grim and miserable December day; my own joy at drawing water was spontaneously interwoven with "the fountain of salvation."

You might call it "metaphorical living." The psalm verses, absorbed into the unconscious and spontaneously resurfacing in the events of daily life, gradually create a different reality in which you live and move. Your life begins to become a place of magical correspondances as you are drawn into the Mystery and experience yourself in its terms.

"You are what you eat," the old saying goes. Mindful of the diet that most of us nonmonastics routinely consume first thing in the morning, along with our coffee and toast, I once challenged members of our spiritual journey group to try for one week replacing the New York Times, CNN, and the morning stock report with a half hour of psalmody and contemplative prayer. Most were astonished at the difference in their attitude and energy and have not gone back to their old routine. "Life is larger when seen through the psalms," one group member commented.

Monasteries are sometimes criticized as an effort to "leave the world." But *what* world, one wonders? As our spiritual journey group discovered, a solicitous addiction to news and information does not necessarily translate into a deeper attunement to the world or an ability to address its needs with clarity and compassion. If the point I've been making about metaphorical living is correct, then we can say that the real business of the monastic journey is exactly the opposite: far from leaving the world, the monk is concerned with a cultivation of those worlds within the inner geography where the subtle meanings, the essential interconnectedness of things, can begin to weave their way into expression in the outer world. Spiritual tradition has universally insisted that it is from the fullness of that other realm that coherence and energy flow into *this* world, sustaining meaningful change. When the eye of the heart is open, you read the patterns written in the depths, and through your own responsiveness, you become a conscious servant of divine becoming.

As a medievalist, I have a story to tell about these inner and outer worlds. One of the all-time medieval bestsellers is an adventure narrative called the *Navigatio Brendani*, or *The Voyage of St. Brendan*.[6] It recounts the saga of a sixth-century Irish monk who set out in a leather boat to discover "the land promised to the saints." He and his monastic crew journeyed for seven years, mostly traveling in circles, until a divine guide finally intervened and pointed the way to their long-desired destination.

As this band travels, they seem to do so in monastic time and space. Virtually all passages are in forty-day increments, the traditional length of liturgical seasons of fasting and feasting. Wherever the crew makes landfall, their first priority is to sing the Divine Office, either with other monks who mysteriously inhabit these outposts or with the birds and beasts who even more mysteriously know the tunes and order of psalmody. Saint Brendan seems to move by celestial way points: Christmas finds him in southern waters (probably among the Azores) celebrating the Eucharist with angelically supplied bread; as Easter approaches, his annual landfall on "the island of sheep" (presumably one of the Faroes) yields up a "spotless lamb" with which to celebrate the paschal mysteries. As he returns each Pentecost to "the island of the birds," the flock swoops down to join him in festival vespers, the psalmody spelled out with all the detail and precision of a liturgical sacramentary book.

Scholars have long been bedeviled by this medieval vision quest and have tried repeatedly to collapse the tension. Is Brendan's voyage an actual account of an early Celtic exploration of the North Atlantic, or is it merely a religious allegory?

In fact, about thirty years ago, an adventurer named Tim Severin became convinced that the voyage of Saint Brendan was an account of an actual Irish landfall on North American shores via the "stepping-stone route" (Ireland to the Hebrides to the Faroes to Iceland to Newfoundland) and set out to prove his thesis by meticulously recreating the voyage from the clues given in the narrative.[7] He copied the leather boat, the clothing worn by the crew, the oars, the sailing rig, the route of the journey, and even the provisioning and tools for hunting and fishing. But the one detail he deliberately declined to copy was the psalmody, even though it was spelled out in the manuscript in exhaustive and insistent detail. This, he evidently felt, was a personal matter, a piece of the medieval mysticism that could safely be set aside.

Severin and his crew eventually managed a landfall on Newfoundland. But that is not where Brendan wound up. Those Irish sailor-monks, by their own account, reached "the land promised to the saints," which, though its physical coordinates may have coincided with Newfoundland, was far more than that barren and rocky outer world. As the manuscript makes clear, the land promised to the saints is reached not only in physical space, but simultaneously in *inner* space through the journey of moral and spiritual purification that prepares the way for the eventual opening

of the eye of the heart. Only through this unitive eye does the land promised to the saints become recognizable—which is why Brendan and his
crew had to circle for seven years before they were finally inwardly prepared to make their landfall. Faith is a legitimate geographical coordinate
on this journey, and the true location of the Promised Land is precisely at
the point Severin and his crew so naively overlooked: at the convergence
of inner and outer worlds found not through collapsing the metaphoric
tension, but by allowing it to become the bridge by which one crosses. As
life is experienced through the metaphors of the psalms, this tension becomes the whole point: the interior journey anchored in the psalms is a
whole different journey and arrives in a wholly different place than a life
not so anchored. As the poet Philip Booth aptly observes, "How you get
there is where you'll arrive."[8]

Just as this was true for Brendan and his crew, so it is for modern-day
monks—and for us as well, as we adopt a practice of contemplative
psalmody as the anchor point of our day. Our world gradually but irrevo-
cably becomes a different place. It's not about piety so much as a new kind
of spiritual intelligence that begins to open up in us as we become fluent
in the time-honored metaphorical language of the psalms.

Again, a medieval Irish monk says it well in a poem titled "To an Old
Psalm Book":

> Seeking the presence of elusive God
> Wandering we stray, but the way is found
> Following the mighty melodies that with you
> Throughout the world abound.
>
> Not ever silent, you bring the world of God
> To all who in the present world abide,
> And then, through you, through finest mesh
> Man's earnest prayer to God is purified.[9]

The hidden wisdom of monastic psalmody is actually very simple. The psalms are indispensable because the heart, in silence, will understand the message encoded there. When absorbed contemplatively, with their various moods and colors, the psalms become that "finest mesh" that both guides and purifies the heart through the dark journey of the unconscious and heralds the way toward the tropological and unitive senses of scripture, through which the kingdom of heaven is recognized as fully alive and present here and now.

While Benedictine monasticism refined the training of the unitive imagination to a high art, that same potential lies in each of us, and as long as yearning continues to reverberate within us, the psalms will continue to perform their age-old work of shaping that yearning into actual seeing.

6

PSALTERS *and* SOURCEBOOKS

I F YOU'VE COME THIS FAR with me in our study of the hidden wisdom of monastic psalmody, hopefully the title of this chapter will raise the next question on your mind. You want to begin your own contemplative use of the psalms, to enter into their wisdom and get to know them better. Where do you get your hands on them?

Simple question, right? Well, not so simple as it first appears. Considering how long the psalms have been around, it probably comes as no surprise to discover that an embarrassment of riches awaits you (1,670 entries under the heading "psalms," according to my most recent online *Books in Print* search.) You'll find any number of translations, editions, and adaptations available, each with its own perspective, strengths, and weaknesses. And that's just counting the *textual* versions, which will be our concern in this chapter; when you add in music as well, the options increase geometrically.

The obvious starting point is in the Bible, of course, but *which* Bible? There was a time not so long ago when the word *Bible* was virtually synonymous with the King James Version, that great spiritual and literary masterpiece that has guided the hearts and souls of English-speaking

Christians for nearly four centuries.[1] For many people, in fact, the King James Version *is* the language of the Bible, and it's well-nigh impossible to conceive of the great scriptural teachings in any other rendition. My grandmother was one of those people, and as a youngster, I was set to the task of memorizing my psalms in King James English, complete with the *thees* and *thous* and *yeas* and *verilys*. Today I'm glad that this discipline was forced on me (I can still call up four psalms in full King James regalia), for there have been many occasions, particularly in pastoral and hospice work, when only the Twenty-third Psalm will do and only in its traditional rendition. It's good to have it by memory:

> The Lord is my sheperd, I shall not want.
> He maketh me to lie down in green pastures.
> He leadeth me beside the still waters.
> He restoreth my soul:
> He leadeth me in the paths of righteousness for
> his name's sake.
> Yea, though I walk through the valley of the
> shadow of death,
> I will fear no evil, for thou art with me.
> Thy rod and thy staff, they comfort me.
> Thou preparest a table before me in the presence
> of mine enemies.
> Thou annointest my head with oil; my cup
> runneth over.
> Surely, goodness and mercy shall follow me all
> the days of my life,
> And I will dwell in the house of the Lord forever.

The past sixty years, however, have seen an abundance of important new translations. Beginning with the Revised Standard Version (RSV) of 1952, an undertaking of the National Council of Churches and decades in the preparation, these new versions reflect the considerable advances that have been made in both scholarship and ecumenical collaboration. The most prominent among today's highly regarded "authorized versions" are the New English Bible (NEB), 1970; New International Version (NIV), 1973; and New Revised Standard Version (NRSV), 1989.

After centuries of doggedly holding to its own course, the Roman Catholic Church entered these new ecumenical waters in the 1960s, contributing the Jerusalem Bible (1966), which has been equally well received in both Catholic and Protestant sectors.[2] More recently the Christian Community Bible, a lively new translation by Roman Catholics in the Philippines, has been gaining much favorable attention not only for its overall literary excellence, but for its social sensitivity that keeps the biblical message of compassionate justice front and center.[3]

While these new bibles are a great improvement in both accuracy and accessibility, there are few that really soar as poetry, particularly singable poetry. Here is the Twenty-third Psalm in its NEB version—technically correct but definitely plodding when compared to the majesty of the King James translation:

> The Lord is my shepherd; I shall want nothing.
>   He makes me lie down in green pastures,
> And leads me beside the waters of peace;
>   He renews life within me,
> And for his name's sake guides me in the right
>   path.
> Even though I walk through a valley dark as
>   death,
> I fear no evil, for thou art with me,
> Thy staff and thy crook are my comfort.
>
> Thou spreadest a table for me in the sight of my
>   enemies;

Thou hast richly bathed my head with oil,
    and my cup runs over.
Goodness and love unfailing, these will follow me
    all the days of my life,
    and I shall dwell in the house of the Lord
    my whole life long.

Favoring impact over precision, evangelical and fundamentalist Christians tend to prefer the Living and Good News bibles with their easy, informal style that gives the reader the feeling of being addressed directly.[4] You can taste a bit of this difference by comparing the opening verses of Psalm 12 in any of the more standardized modern translations with their equivalent in the "relaxed fit" version of The Living Bible:

Help me, Lord, for there is no godly one left;
The faithful have vanished from among us.

Everyone speaks falsely with his neighbor;
With a smooth tongue they speak from a double
    heart.
                        —*The Book of Common Prayer*

Lord! Help! Godly men are fast disappearing. Where in the world can dependable men be found? Everyone deceives and flatters and lies. There is no sincerity left.

                        —*The Living Bible*

It's no small challenge to come up with translations that are both accurate and compelling. When you add yet a third desideratum that the translation also be *singable*—in other words, metrically straightforward enough to support the psalm tones we'll shortly be learning to chant—you begin to appreciate why the Benedictine monastic tradition clung so long and steadfastly to its Latin psalmody, which for all its shortcomings in the contemporary intelligibility department remains unsurpassed in its poetic concision and beauty.

Psalters

In addition to being included in the Bible, the psalms have traditionally been made available in stand-alone volumes called psalters. That tradition continues today, and in fact, it's in these contemporary psalters rather than the Bible itself that you're most likely to come upon good, workable translations suitable for both lectio divina and contemplative chanting.

One of my favorite psalters is found right within the pages of the Book of Common Prayer, available in the pews of any Episcopal church (you can also purchase it in most bookstores).[5] The translations are formal but fluid and lend themselves easily to chanting, as you'll see shortly. As a further support to contemplative practice, you'll find the psalms already arranged into daily morning and evening readings, allowing you to cover the entire psalter in the course of a month.

Among Catholic monastics, the Grail Psalms are still highly in favor. Originally developed for liturgical use as the Church shifted from its Latin ritual to the vernacular, they now occupy pride of place as the libretto for much of contemporary Roman Catholic psalmody. In addition to the various chanted versions (some of which we'll be meeting later in this book), these psalms also exist as a text-alone psalter.[6] This unpretentious little book is the version most likely to be put out for vigils in communities where the night psalms are recited rather than chanted. The Grail Psalms are straightforward both poetically and metrically, which makes them a good basic libretto. Their earlier weak points—occasional awkward or stilted phrasing and a few glaring lapses in the inclusive language department—have largely been corrected in more recent editions.

We spoke in chapter 4 about the problems and perils vis-à-vis the psalms and political correctness. For some contemporary translators, the violence and religious intolerance of the psalms simply cannot be left unchallenged, and in place of translations, what we really have are dynamic paraphrases, preserving the spirit of the original but within a contemporary context.

One of the earliest and still most popular contributions to this field is *A Book of Psalms* by widely acclaimed poet Stephen Mitchell.[7] Mitchell deals with the most problematic of the cursing psalms by the path of least resistance: he simply eliminates them! (His psalter, therefore, is technically only a partial one.) But you'll find the majority of the psalms presented here in translations that do honor both to the poetry and to the timeless wisdom of the psalm tradition.

In more recent years, a welcome newcomer to the field has been Nan Merrill's *Psalms for Praying: An Invitation to Wholeness.*[8] Merrill is a contemplative with a huge heart and an eclectic mind; for decades she has supported her hermit solitude through a monthly broadside called "Friends of Silence," published from her home in rural Vermont. During her long years of living, breathing, and praying the psalms, her perception of them inevitably began to shift. More and more, she came to hear their cries of yearning addressed not to a distant Lord God but to the Beloved, as intimate and gentle as her own heart.

"The psalms of the Hebrew Scriptures often reflect a patriarchal society based on fear and guilt that projects evil and sin onto outer enemies," she writes in the preface to her psalter. Her intention in *Psalms for Praying*, she explains, is "to reflect the reciprocity of divine love that opens the heart to forgiveness, reconciliation, and healing."[9]

Psalms for Praying became an instant hit with many contemplative prayer groups; the bookstore for Contemplative Outreach, Thomas Keating's huge Centering Prayer network, has trouble keeping copies in stock. You'll see why when you compare Merrill's translation of Psalm 134 with any standard version. In the Episcopal Psalter, this very short psalm reads as follows:

> Behold now, bless the Lord, all you servants of
>   the Lord,
>   you that stand by night in the house of the
>   Lord.
>
> Lift up your hands in the holy place and bless the
>   Lord;
>   The Lord who made heaven and earth bless
>   you out of Zion.

Now look at what Nan Merrill writes:

> Come, bask in the light of Love,
>   all you who would serve
>   the Divine Plan!
> Lift up your hands to the Holy One
>   singing songs of praise!
> Bow down and receive blessing from
>   the Giver of Life!
>   All praise be to You,
>   whose Love created heaven and earth!

The opening verses to her version of Psalm 23 reveal some of her characteristic touches, such as addressing God directly as "You" (rather than making statements *about* God) and her emphasis that the very essence of God is love:

> O my Beloved, you are my shepherd,
>   I shall not want;

You bring me to green pastures
for rest
and lead me beside still waters
renewing my spirit,
You restore my soul.
You lead me in the path of
goodness
to follow Love's way.

When the challenge to love is fierce, as in Psalm 137 ("By the rivers of Babylon we sat down and wept"), she sets the literal text aside altogether and instead pens what can only be described as a response from mystical love to the deep inner pain of this psalm:

Plunge into the Ocean of Love
where heart meets Heart,
Where sorrows are comforted, and
wounds are mended.
There, melodies of sadness mingle with
dolphin songs of joy;
Past fears dissolve in deep harmonic
tones,
the future—pure mystery.
For eternal moments lived in total
surrender
glide smoothly over troubled
waters.

Hide not from Love, O friends,
sink not into the sea of despair,
the mire of hatred.
Awaken, O my heart, that I drown not
in fear!

Too long have I sailed where'ere
the winds have blown!
Drop anchor!
O, Heart of all hearts, set a
clear course,
that I might follow!
Guide me to the Promised Shore!

Many have commented that reading the psalms through the eyes of Nan Merrill is like reading them through those of the poet Rumi. Moving beyond time and cultural conditioning, she speaks to what is most universal and yet most personal in the human experience.

Another excellent recent resource for contemporary psalmody is *Ancient Songs Sung Anew* by Lynn Bauman.[10] Acknowledging that his project had its starting point in a time of deep personal turmoil and suffering, he set out to discover what the psalms would sound like if prayed in words that expressed the conditions and experiences of contemporary life. The result is a psalter acutely tuned to the reality of human loss and psychological pain. Drawing on his more than a decade of studying and teaching in the Middle East, his psalms also reflect the influence of the ancient Wisdom schools (with which Jesus would have been well acquainted)[11] and their teachings on the transmutation of personal pain through spiritual surrender and nonattachment. While his translations are not particularly singable, they provide fertile ground for lectio divina.

This brief tour of translations merely scratches the surface, but it does give you some idea of what's out there. Depending on how deeply you want to plunge into your contemplative psalmody, it may be useful to keep several versions on the shelf to check and compare as you work with the texts in lectio divina. But as several of my monk friends have commented, the very best kind of psalter is a well-worn one! As in all spiritual practice, establishing a regular routine helps you to move from purely mental perception into those deeper waters we've been talking about. No matter what version you use, the psalms will continue to be a catalyst for awakening conscience and inner sight.

The Numbering Hiccup

Before we leave the textual aspects of psalmody, it's important to clear up one lingering source of confusion, which I alluded to in chapter 1. From the fifth century until well into the twentieth, the Roman Catholic scriptural tradition was based on the Vulgate, the magnificent work of Saint Jerome. The word *vulgate* shares the same root as *vulgar*; it designates the translation of the Bible into the vernacular of the day (that is, Latin), based largely on the Greek New Testament and what's known as the Greek Septuagint version of the Old Testament scriptures.

Ten centuries later, when the headwaters of Protestantism began to arise in the form of new translations of the Bible, the new scholar-reformers went directly back to the Hebrew scriptures. This information would simply be a matter of scholarly trivia except for one very important consequence. The Hebrew version divides Psalm 9 into two psalms (9 and 10), while the Vulgate-Septuagint tradition keeps it as a single psalm. As a result, Roman Catholic and Protestant numberings are off by one from Psalm 9 onward.[12] Things don't come back together again until the very end, when Psalm 147 (in Protestant usage) becomes two psalms in Roman Catholic usage (146 and 147) and the divergent paths rejoin.

Today that dissonance is beginning to fade. As the weight of biblical scholarship has consolidated around the greater accuracy of the Hebrew version, Roman Catholic usage has begun to fall into line. Beginning with the Jerusalem Bible (1996), you'll see the "standardized" numberings in use—sometimes accompanied by the earlier Vulgate designations in parentheses. (We will be using the standardized numbering throughout this book).

But old traditions die hard, particularly when they've been lived and prayed as deeply as monastic psalmody. If for forty or more years of monastic life you've known "The Lord is my shepherd" as Psalm 22 or "Shout with joy to the Lord, all ye lands" as Psalm 99, it's hard to unlearn these deep habits of the heart. In many Catholic monasteries, the old numberings remain unofficially but affectionately in use—a good thing to keep in mind if you're on retreat. And if you happen to fall in love with Gregorian chant and manage to get your hands on a copy of the *Liber Usualis*, then you'll need to be conversant with the old numbering system, since that's how all the psalms are identified. Beneath the surface, it's all the same heart.

 *Part Two*

CHANTING
the PSALMS

 7

FINDING
YOUR VOICE

FROM TIME TO TIME I try an experiment with groups gathering for a weekend workshop on contemplative chanting and psalmody. As we sit in a circle, I ask each person to introduce himself or herself to the person sitting on the right with the greeting, "Hello, my name is . . ."

Not a problem. I remember one particular group, about half of them clergy, who rose to the occasion with gusto, greeting their neighbors with full, hearty voices and obvious command of their presentational skills. As the exercise came full circle, I was greeted by a woman priest who introduced herself with a commanding voice nearly in the tenor range: "Hello, my name is Sarah."

Then I introduced the plot twist: "Okay, let's do that same exercise again—only this time, *chant* the "Hello, my name is . . ." I demonstrated on a monotone chant, and off we went.

The results ranged from hilarious to poignant, depending on your take. It was a total unmasking of what we'd just heard. Some voices that had seemed shy and retiring when speaking proved to have a beautiful, resonant timbre, and people looked at each other in newfound appreciation.

Some of the heartiest of the verbal greeters turned out to be all bluff, struggling to find a wavering little note, as if suddenly exposed. The magesterial Sarah quavered out her "Hello, I'm Sarah" in a breathy little soprano, somewhere between a tone and a whisper.

What had happened? Whatever it was, it's the essence of this book. The greatest challenge in sacred chanting is the same as its greatest opportunity: it strips away the masks and forces us to work with what's real.

True Voice, True Self

The word *psalm*, of course, means "song." Technically there is no such thing, then, as a spoken psalm. That would be an oxymoron, like a two-wheeled tricycle. But if psalms are really songs, that means we need to sing them. Which brings us to the awkward and embarrassing matter of making friends with our singing voice.

It's sad that we North Americans live in what has largely become a nonsinging culture, particularly in recent decades. Even in our own parents' and grandparents' memories, hymn sings were still a common part of community life, and Sunday mornings could be counted on to raise the rafters. Around the world this tradition still continues honorably, but in our own fast-paced society, the opportunities for people simply to get together and sing have all but died out. The hootenannies of the 1960s were pretty much the last hurrah for this most ancient and basic of all communication arts.

Yes, people who love to sing still find their way to choirs, and the church choir is still a venerable institution of Christian life. But in this age of specialization, church choirs are often semiprofessional or even professional organizations of people who know how to read music and deliver the goods on Sunday morning. In churches where the psalms are chanted at all, you're more likely to find them chanted *to* the congregation than *by* the congregation.

When it comes to contemplative chanting, we're into a whole new set of challenges. More often than not, the contemplatively minded folks within a congregation are not the same contingent as those who are in the choir. As a matter of fact, when I first embarked on my project of reintroducing chanting into Christian contemplative practice, my biggest resistance came from the hard-core meditators who let it be known that they had become contemplatives precisely so they *wouldn't* have to sing.

One woman in our Centering Prayer group in British Columbia was particularly adamant in her opposition to any form of chanted psalmody. She maintained that it disrupted her silence. Finally, when challenged by another group member, she revealed a bit more of the story. Back in an elementary school music class when she was seven or eight years old, the teacher had stopped the singing midstream and asked distastefully, "What's that buzzing noise? Oh, it's *you*, Stella!" Fifty years later, Stella remembered this incident as clear as day and wanted nothing to do with any practice that would ever take her near that humiliation again. I have found that the ranks of Christian meditators tend to be populated in remarkably high proportion by men who were ridiculed during their voice change or youngsters who were instructed to "just lip-synch" during the Christmas pageant or school operetta.

I suspect (at least I hope) that there may be some special corner of hell reserved for such grade-school music vigilantes. For the damage done is not just to our instrument of musical expression and exploration, but to that of spiritual expression and exploration as well.

In chapter 3, I spoke of how, when we work with our voice, we work with the core elements out of which the world came into being and through which it is sustained: breath, tone, intentionality, and community. These four elements are actually our sacred tools for plumbing the mystery of creation with something other than our indefatigable Western minds. It's a whole different experience to connect to the biblical Word with your breath and tone rather than just reading or speaking it. A whole different part of your being is engaged, and a whole different intelligence and perceptivity flows from this engagement.

I have learned this lesson the hard way many times over while preparing a Sunday sermon. Though I know full well that the classic methodology of lectio divina advises always to read the scriptural passage aloud before you begin to work with it, I've often cheated on this instruction, simply skimming the text with my eyes as I begin to shape my thoughts into a sermon. Nine times out of ten, when I finally read the passage out loud during the proclamation of the Gospel on Sunday morning, I hear exactly the phrase or innuendo that I should have preached on but that escaped my reading eye.

Virtually all spiritual paths begin their training with breath and tone—conscious breathing, following the breath, vibrating the mantra—and for good reason: these are the actual tools and technologies for engaging and energizing our more subtle inner being. In chapter 3, we saw how Gregorian chant developed this training into a high art, but the same principle underlies all sacred chanting, no matter how simple.

There is an even more important factor at work here, however. As I've worked with people's voices within a spiritual context, I have come to see more and more that true voice is closely intertwined with true self—in other words, the essential manifestation of who we are. That's why people feel so exposed, so vulnerable in an exercise such as I described at the beginning of this chapter. When we sing out of who we truly are—connected to our breath, with a tone that is neither forced nor constricted—we are essentially coming from the marrow of ourselves. It's a very vulnerable kind of activity.

It's easy to fake our speaking voice. We can manufacture hearty tones, imposing authority, or superficial cordiality. The speaking voice also quickly takes on all the artificialities and constrictions of our personality—our hidden fears and dishonesties, our conditioning, and the stress we routinely and often unconsciously carry within us. To be sure, there are voice teachers who can help you to fake your singing voice as well. There are a variety of techniques that will increase your volume or allow you to "belt out" a song, nearly all of them involving some strain or constriction in your throat. But a good voice teacher will be much more interested in freeing you up so that whatever tone you make is clear, honest, unforced, and supported. Then you will be singing from your authentic raw material, which in the long run, is the only sustainable approach in both music and the spiritual life.

Some Starting Affirmations

As we now move into the practical part of this book, I'm aware that you might be picturing yourself as one of those people in the circle I spoke of earlier, wondering what will happen when it's your turn to chant, "Hello, my name is . . ." Perhaps you're comfortable with simple solo singing, perhaps not. Either way, I'd like to begin with a few affirmations that will be the basis for our work together and that I hope will ease your initial performance anxiety.

First and most important is the affirmation that your real singing voice is beautiful. No, I'm not talking about operatic style here or suggesting that you're a Pavarotti in disguise. But because your true singing voice is so closely connected to your authentic self, and because this authentic self is nothing less than the glory of God written in you as your *being*, you can relax and enjoy the ride. Whether your tone is big or small, reedy or clear, high or low, it is the perfect and (more to the point) the only instrument at your disposal.

Second, making this instrument perform at optimum capacity is not so much a matter of adding on (volume, vibrato, and so on) as of taking away: taking away the strain, the constriction, and the anxiety. These three goals are largely accomplished simply by staying connected to your breath and your tone. When you do this, all the while listening as well as you can to others around you, your voice will work perfectly well in nine cases out of ten. Building more volume and vocal range is mainly a matter of building confidence and mastering a few basic techniques of voice production. But for our purposes in contemplative chanting, a small, open, connected voice will do just fine.

Finally—and again, because of this close relationship between true voice and true self—working with your voice in chanting is an absolutely marvelous way to deepen the process of self-inquiry, exploring the material of your essential being and the blockages and constrictions in your personality. If you're willing to use it this way, it's an opportunity to move beyond egoic performance anxiety and learn more about the creature you truly and magnificently are. So with those affirmations, let's begin.

Warming Up

This book is not really designed to be a singing manual, but a small bit of musical common sense will get you started on the right foot. Singers almost always begin rehearsals with a vocal warm-up, and if you're easing yourself back into singing after a time away (perhaps decades!), a warm-up is definitely the place to start. The accompanying CD contains a full vocal warm-up you can sing along with, but first let me talk you through the process. [CD track 1] ⦿

Begin simply by standing up (or sitting up straight in a hard-backed chair). Sense your feet on the ground. Let your head rest comfortably on your shoulders, not drooping your head down or tilting it back. Check out the usual points of tension: shoulders, jaws, the back of your head, around your eyes. Relax! If you want to, you can swing your arms or roll your head around on your neck to shake out some of that tightness.

Now take some deep breaths—not by moving your shoulders up and down in the "chest breathing" we so easily fall into in the West, but in the way you did naturally from the time of your birth, breathing from your diaphragm. That's the muscle in the very center of your torso (just below your lungs), where both your breath and the bottom of your vocal column are anchored. It relaxes and expands as you take in air and contracts as you exhale. If you like, you can place your hands over your abdomen and feel the grounded, steady rhythm of its expansion and contraction; if you look at yourself in a mirror, you'll notice that your shoulders remain level.

Take several breaths this way, breathing in and out steadily with a rhythm that is unforced and natural for you.

Now, with your attention focused in your diaphragm, start to make a "hmm" sound in a comfortable middle range. Breathe in and out with your "hmm" a few times, then shift to "ah."

As you sing your "ah," see if you can keep it grounded in your breath. Picture yourself as a cello string that is attached at the bottom to your diaphragm, and at the top to the roof of your mouth (which incidentally, is a perfect resonating and amplifying chamber: your own little Romanesque chapel). Enjoy the resonance of your tone as it vibrates along the full length of that imaginary column. Don't try to make a loud sound, just one that stays connected.

Virtually all ugliness and tension in singing is created by constricting this natural resonating column. If you sing only with your mouth, your tone will be breathy; if you force from your throat (a common shortcut used to manufacture a "big sound"), your tone will be shrill or strident. But when you keep the full vocal column vibrating and realize that even (in fact, especially) high notes have to be made bottom up, not top down, then you will sing with the support you need. "Support your tone!" is an admonishment frequently given by voice teachers and choir directors; it means to keep your singing grounded and "fully aerated" in your diaphragm breathing.

CHANTING
THE PSALMS

With your voice warmed up and ready to go, it's time now to take our first practice run at actually chanting a psalm. For this maiden voyage, let's use the first eight verses of Psalm 34, from the Book of Common Prayer:

   1   I will bless the Lord at all times;*
        his praise shall ever be in my mouth.

   2   I will glory in the Lord;*
        let the humble hear and rejoice.

   3   Proclaim with me the greatness of the Lord; *
        let us exalt his Name together.

   4   I sought the Lord, and he answered me*
        and delivered me out of all my terror.

   5   Look upon him and be radiant,*
        and let not your faces be ashamed.

   6   I called in my affliction and the Lord heard me*
        and saved me from all my troubles.

   7   The angel of the Lord encompasses those who
             fear him,*
        and he will deliver them.

   8   Taste and see that the Lord is good;*
        happy are they who trust in him!

Begin by reading out loud, just as if you were practicing to read this psalm during a church service. Note how you bring your reading to life, shaping the phrases and word sense so that your reading communicates meaning. In the first line, for example, you might decide to put your major emphasis on the word *Lord* so that the whole line moves toward that climax. Or you might prefer to emphasize the word *bless*, giving a slightly different spin to the words. Either way is fine; these individual sensitivities to meaning and innuendo are what make a reading lively and engaging. The amazing thing is that most adults can manage this completely intuitively. The eye-voice-meaning synapses have become so deeply ingrained that the process happens naturally and virtually spontaneously. You simply have to get out of your own way and go with what you know. No problem, right?

Well, now it's time to do the same exercise I described at the beginning of this chapter. I want you to go back to these eight verses and *chant* them. In other words, simply pick a pitch that feels comfortable to you (maybe that "ah" sound we worked on earlier) and bring your voice to the spoken words. Listen to the accompanying CD to hear how I do this. [CD track 2] ◉

Congratulations! You've now officially chanted your first psalm. It's that simple. Once you have the hang of it, you can chant anything and everything in that same fashion: the Gospel, the Lord's Prayer, the Passion narrative on Good Friday, the canon of the Mass. In fact, that's how liturgical texts were traditionally delivered in churches before the age of amplification (the chanting helped the sound to carry). The practice continues even today in many cathedrals and "high" liturgical churches, particularly during solemn celebrations. But as you're gaining confidence with this art form, you can have some fun as well. Members of our contemplative journey group have honed their skills (and been the life of the party) chanting Dr. Seuss, computer manuals, and IRS forms!

A bit earlier I asked you to pay attention to the process that allows you to read expressively. You intuitively scanned the line, paying attention to the pattern of stressed and unstressed syllables within individual words and to the overall line sense, then you arranged the rise and fall of your voice to match that sense. This is exactly the process you'll be following as you chant the psalms. The particular chant style we'll primarily be working with in this book is called "nonmensural," which means that it doesn't have measures and a steady beat. Unlike some styles of chanting, it doesn't lend itself to being accompanied by a drum; instead, the rhythm and liveliness is created by the natural meter and impulse of the line itself.

This is an all-important principle to learn from the start; it's what I was referring to earlier in the sacred aspect of intentionality. What you pay attention to, you energize; what you withdraw attention from loses intensity, interest, and usually pitch. Right now, before you begin to complicate matters with melodies (the psalm tones we'll be considering shortly), learn to energize your chant line by singing sense. With this lesson under your belt, all the rest will go well.

Staying on Pitch

As part of the performance anxiety turf (along with the fear of making a tone in the first place), many people are convinced that they are tone-deaf. By this, they usually mean that they can't match pitch; if they hear a note sung, they can't sing it back. Like my friend Stella, they live in dread of being singled out for their monotone "buzzing."

In point of fact, only a very small percentage of people who think they're tone-deaf turn out to be so. In the vast majority of cases, the problem improves dramatically when the fear factor is resolved. All fear constricts, and the fear of humiliation constricts utterly, affecting the ears as much as the voice itself. Once you relax, the tone deafness problem is usually resolved by learning a few basic techniques: listening, learning to place your voice, and finding the notes by their inner feel. All of these things can be mastered fairly easily; it's mostly a matter of getting used to your own instrument.

Keeping a note on pitch is a slightly different issue, and one that will be concerning us throughout this book, just as it concerns all choirs. We've just practiced basic monophonic chanting, and it may be reassuring for you to know that what we just did in chanting Psalm 34 will actually carry you through about 80 percent of the chanting we'll be doing in this book, which is singing on a simple one-note reciting tone.

Easy, isn't it? Once you've found the note, you just keep it going? Well, yes and no. In fact, choirs seem to go flat (lose pitch) on the reciting tone as much as on the moving melodies. The secret is that you have to re-energize each note (even if it's the same note over and over) by keeping it connected to your breath and your intentionality. If you go out to lunch, the pitch will get slack and drift downhill. Tonal accuracy is about 95 percent attention.

For that relatively small population who simply cannot hear and match the pitch, all is not lost. Certainly what note you sing on makes no difference when you're chanting by yourself; your notes can be whatever they please. Even in a group, if it's a compassionate group (and aren't contemplatives supposed to be compassionate?), you will be able participate meaningfully as long as you remember the lesson that monk taught me: "If you can't hear the person next to you, you're singing too loud." I have searched the Rule of Saint Benedict diligently and find no demerits given for an inability to keep the pitch. Deep listening and humility will carry you most of the way. In monastic training, of course, that's the goal. But even as a choir singer, you may be astonished to discover how far these same spiritual techniques will go toward freeing up your voice.

At any rate, in this choir, all are welcome, buzzing or not. The most

8

SUZUKI
PSALMODY

W HEN YOU USE THE SUZUKI METHOD to learn a musical instrument, you start right off playing by ear rather than sight-reading.
So when I talk about "Suzuki psalmody," I mean learning to sing a simple
psalm tone by ear, without first having to master the more complicated
musical notation that puts some people off.

A psalm tone, simply means the tune to which you sing the psalm.
When you see *tone*, think *tune*. This is the first of several items of basic terminology that we'll be getting acquainted with during this lesson.

In the last chapter, you learned to chant a psalm on a single note. If
you find yourself getting bored with that and want to try something a bit
fancier, you can move on to a very simple step-up, step-down arrangement, still entirely by ear.

In many modern psalters designed for congregational use, you'll find
the verses individually numbered and divided clearly into two half verses,
known as versicles. The Episcopal Psalter uses this arrangement throughout and makes this division point flagrantly obvious by notating it with an
asterisk (*). Using the asterisk as your guide, you simply step *up* one note
on the last accented syllable before the asterisk, then step *down* again on

the last stressed syllable of the line. (Syllables that are stressed are set in boldface type.)

If we use Psalm 34 again to demonstrate this method, the first three verses would go like this: [CD track 3] ⊙

I will bless the Lord at all **times**;* (step up)
his praise shall ever be in my **mouth**. (step down)

I will glory in the **Lord**;* (step up)
let the humble hear and re**joice**. (step down)

Proclaim with me the greatness of the **Lord**;*
    (step up)
let us exalt his name to**gether**. (step down)

There's a general stylistic preference to put the step-up or step-down on the last *stressed* syllable rather than simply the last syllable, particularly if the final word is a short pronoun like *me, you,* or *him.* So in the following verse, which says, "I sought the Lord and he answered me," you would sing, "he **answered** me," not "he answered **me**." A few verses later, when the psalm says, "I called in my affliction and the Lord heard me," you would sing, "the Lord **heard** me," not "the Lord heard **me**." It just sounds better. You'll figure a lot of this out just by common sense.

Choirs, in fact, spend a lot of time pondering over these details, and there is often no clear-cut right and wrong. Individual choices based on custom or personal taste comprise what is known as a "house style."

In working through this exercise, you will also have acquired two more pieces of chant nomenclature. The monotone note you sang for most of the versicle is called the "reciting tone," for reasons which are presumably obvious. The step-up or step-down note that brings the versicle to its close is called the "cadence tone."

For those of you who can read music, what we're singing in this step-up, step-down formula is a major second. Written down musically, it looks like this:

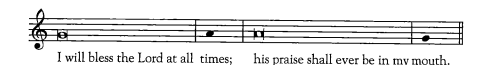
I will bless the Lord at all times;   his praise shall ever be in my mouth.

Using this simple method, you can sing virtually any psalm in the psalter that lends itself (or can be wrestled into) couplet format—that is, two-line pairs. In fact, I know a couple who did just that. An Episcopal priest and his wife, neither of them trained musicians, attended a workshop I gave on Benedictine spiritual practice and decided to take Divine Office back to their home parish. Day in and day out for four years, sometimes alone and sometimes joined by other parishoners, they gathered at seven in the morning and seven in the evening to sing the psalms appointed for the day using this same step-up, step-down formula. It was a remarkable act of commitment and trust that even simple things, done with care, can work well.

What about psalms that seem to want to be in three-line verses, as is true with many of the Grail Psalms? In such cases, a standard practice is to sing the first verse entirely on a monotone, then begin the step-up, step-down arrangement on the second verse. Monastic psalmody makes frequent use of this simple way of "stretching" a psalm tone; where it's in use, you'll usually find the line to be sung on a monotone designated by a dash.

A Different Way of Stepping Up and Down

The step-up, step-down (or major second) arrangement we've already discussed has a cheerful, upbeat feeling to it. But as we've seen, psalms have many moods and many colors. When the color of a psalm feels darker and more serious, it may sound a bit "off" if you sing it in the major second formula. So here's an alternative psalm tone; it's just as simple but distinctly more somber in mood. It's called a minor second: a half-step, rather than a full step, up and down. Here in Psalm 130, a very serious and earnest psalm, is a good example of when you might want to use it: [CD track 4] ⊚

Out of the depths have I called to you, O Lord;
Lord, hear my **voice**;*
　　let your ears consider well the voice of my
　　pleading;

If you, Lord, were to note what is done **amiss**,*
　　O Lord, who could **stand**?

For there is forgiveness with **you**;*[1]
　　therefore you shall be feared.

I wait for the Lord, my soul **waits** for him;*
　　in his word is my **hope**.

My soul waits for the Lord
more than watchmen for the **morning**,*
　　more than watchmen for the **morning**.

O Israel, wait for the **Lord**,*
　　for with the Lord there is **mercy**.

With him there is plenteous re**demp**tion;*
　　and he shall redeem Israel from all their **sins**.

If you agree that this second tone sounds more appropriate to the mood of the text, you've just gotten the gist of the whole notion of plainsong "modes," another foundational piece of chant vocabulary. The basic idea is that different arrangements of half-steps and whole steps create distinctly different musical moods, like a musical color palette. That first step-up, step-down formula, based on the major second, created a cheerful, somewhat singsongy mood; the second one, based on the minor second, created a more mysterious and plaintive atmosphere.

For contemporary Westerners, accustomed to the diatonic scale of the piano (do-re-mi-fa-sol-la-ti-do) and the classical music theory that is based on it, this whole notion of modes takes a bit of getting used to. We tend to think in terms of keys rather than modes, and "major" and "minor" are all that remain of a once extremely sophisticated and still more ancient and universal way of organizing the ear.[2] In classic Gregorian chant, there were eight modes, which are identified in the *Liber Usualis* by the corresponding Roman numeral at the beginning of the chant. Looking at the number, you would know immediately which pattern of whole and half-steps to apply.[3]

If this all sounds a bit esoteric—and standard chant manuals do have a way of making the subject of modes overly complex—remember that you have already experienced the essence of the matter in our simple Suzuki chanting. For example, in the exercise we just did, if we called the major second pattern "mode one" and the minor second pattern "mode two," all I'd have to do would be to say, "Now let's sing Psalm 34 in mode two," and you'd know what to do. Turn to track 5 on your CD to hear how it goes. [CD track 5] ◉

In this book, we will not be spending much time with the classic plainsong modes. They are really essential only within the genre of Gregorian chant, and as we'll be seeing, there's a whole wide world of chant out there beyond the Gregorian horizon. But from this brief example, you'll at least have some basic understanding of what they're all about.

Stretching Your Ear

So far, so good. Now we'll add a bit more musical complexity that's still well within the capacity of your Suzuki ear. If the step-up, step down formula begins to sound a bit klunky to you, whether it's major or minor, here's a very graceful psalm tone that will work well for almost any psalm—kind of your "basic black" of the psalm tone world. I call it the "Anglican tone" because it has the flavor of contemporary Anglican plainsong. Again, we'll try it out using Psalm 130. Listen to it first on the CD. [CD track 6] ⊙ In musical notation, it looks like this:

Out of the depths have I called to you; O Lord; Lord hear my voice.*

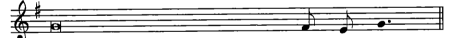

Let your ears consider well the voice of my   sup - pli - cation.

The first versicle (before the asterisk) is sung entirely on a monotone. The second is a bit more complicated. Between the reciting tone and the cadence tone are added two very short notes, called "passing tones." They are apportioned to the two syllables immediately preceding the cadence tone (which, you remember, is the last accented syllable in the line.) The syllables following the cadence tone, if any—such as the "ing" of *pleading*—are sung on the same note as the cadence tone.

How do you know where to put the passing tones? At first this may appear challenging, and you may be tempted to try to parse it out in advance. Don't! Again, this is one of the mysteries of the ear-mind-voice connection: if you don't try to figure it out, you'll automatically know how to do it. Thinking about it uses the wrong part of your brain—like trying to balance on a bicycle by staring down at the front wheel or play the piano while looking at your fingers. If you trust your ear and the natural abilities of scansion that we already encountered in the preceding chapter, you can do the matchup spontaneously and without stumbling. I've tried this experiment time and again, even with raw amateurs, and they're amazed to discover that somehow they just pick it up.

In fact, a good deal of the unnecessary difficulty in learning to chant actually comes from an over-reliance on the musical notation. This is not just a question of sight-reading ability, but of entirely different systems of intelligence being called into play, and the underlying principle has important implications for contemplative practice. The visual cues will tend to engage that more mental part of your brain—the analyzing, calculating, figuring-out left brain. Trusting your ears will engage your right brain and put you in touch with that more fluid, integrated heart-knowing part that reads by picking up the patterns. In fact, it is only through engaging this dimension that your chanting will become truly contemplative. Remember that those earliest monastic chanters did their psalmody entirely from memory—without the luxury of a written psalter—ensuring that the whole experience would be processed according to that deeper way of knowing. It's not by accident that a synonym for *memorizing* is "learning by heart."

My recommendation, then, would be not to rush too quickly through this chapter in a desire to get on to more "advanced" material. Take this most recent psalm tone, which is a beautiful, serviceable workhorse, and chant through the entire Psalter, allowing the pattern to become deeply ingrained. Stretch your ability to match the passing tones to their respective syllables completely by ear. If you like, you can also play with this simple variation: [CD track 7]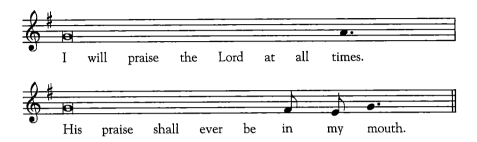

I will praise the Lord at all times.

His praise shall ever be in my mouth.

The more you become accustomed to working entirely by ear, the more quickly you'll be able to pick up the simple, written psalm tones I'll be introducing in the following chapters without getting tangled up in mental operations. You'll also be practicing a skill that will stand you in good stead when you go on retreat, for in many monastic choirs, all you'll be given for your psalmody is the text itself, with some small squiggles above or below the words to show you how the pointing goes (that is, where to put the passing and cadence tones). It's useful—as well as extremely satisfying—to be able to pick up the tune by ear.

Organum

Here's another simple "Suzuki" exercise that will give you an instant medieval cathedral sound. All it requires is at least two people who can basically stay on pitch. Let's return to Psalm 34 to demonstrate.

One person chants the verse on a monotone:

I will bless the Lord at all times
his praise shall ever be in my mouth.

The second person sings exactly the same tune—in this case, the monotone—but either a fourth below it or a fifth above. For those of you who don't read music and need to parse this out on a keyboard, that means go down four whole steps (four white keys) or up five whole steps. For example, if the first person is singing on the note C, either four down or five up will land the second person on the note G, which is the first natural overtone of C. Turn to track 8 on your CD to hear how this sounds. [CD track 8] ⊚

There are wonderful riches to be had in this simplest of all forms of harmony. First, it creates a beautiful, mysterious effect that is very medieval, since up until the twelfth century, all harmony was based on this "quartal" (open fifth) harmony known. Second, it is a stable and comfortable singing position that will tend to stay in tune because the natural resonance of that open fifth serves as a kind of harmonic glue, anchoring and even improving the pitch.

You can have great fun with this trick in your contemplative prayer group or church choir. Chant the Lord's Prayer in organum. Or for a wild sound, try the psalm tone we just worked on in organum. Listen to the results on track 9 of your CD. [CD track 9] ⊚

Certain passages in Gregorian chant lend themselves to organum as well, and where it works, the effect is beyond sublime. In fact, it was a memorable rendition of Gregorian organum more than forty years ago that probably accounts for a good deal of my subsequent journey into the medieval world, not to mention the contemplative world. While still a teenager, I had the opportunity to attend the New York Pro Musica's historic reconstruction of the twelfth-century liturgical drama *The Play of Herod*. In the final verses of the Gregorian *Te Deum* ("We Praise You, O God"), which served as the play's candlelight recessional, the choir suddenly burst into double-octave organum. For a youngster who had grown up in Protestant America to the music of Elvis Presley and the Beach Boys, this sudden total immersion in "the music of the spheres" was a mystical homecoming I will never forget.

A Work of the Heart

As I implied earlier, singing by ear is foundational to all contemplative chanting. Just because this chapter is basic, don't think that it's less important than what follows or that the goal is to be able to work as quickly as possible toward sight-singing notation. The goal is actually to be able to sing notation with the same effortless grace as your Suzuki psalmody, not getting thrown off by the left-brain processing mode that will be engaged as soon as you start working with the visual symbolism. As in acting, the real craft begins once you're "off the book."

9

READING SIMPLE
PSALM NOTATION

A S A MEDIEVAL MUSICOLOGIST, I can attest that the earliest examples of musical notation do not appear before the ninth century, and
they are a far cry from the elegant Gregorian calligraphy that has become
synonymous in most people's minds with the medieval chant tradition.
These earliest specimens of written notation look like little squiggles
above the words in the manuscript—small, upward pointing slashes to indicate an ascending musical line, dots to show that a note is elongated
(held for a longer period of time), or a mark above a note to show when
to move from the reciting tone.

If you've been working on Psalm 34 from our last chapter, chances are
that you may have made a few similar notations in your own psalter as a
visual memory jog—"pointing the psalm," as we called it. Not only is
pointing the earliest known form of notation, but it keeps reinventing itself as the most universal and basic way of remembering how the words
and music match up. Even at many monasteries today, you'll encounter
the psalms for the Divine Office in text-only version, with essentially
these same little squiggles to guide you. Here's a typical example from
Saint Benedict's Monastery:

I thank you, Lord, with âll <u>my heart</u>,
 you have heard the wôrds of mý mouth.

In the presence of the angels I will blêss you.
 I will adore before your hôly témple.

I thank you for your faithfulness ând love
 which excel all we êver knéw <u>of you</u>.

On the day I called, you ânswered;
 you increased the strêngth of my soul.

When you find yourself in this situation, you have an opportunity to draw on your Suzuki skills. Listen carefully to the psalm tone until you have it by ear. In monastic tradition, psalms are nearly always sung antiphonally—that is, alternating between one side of the room and the other, or between a solo cantor and the choir—so you'll have time to listen when you're not singing. Simply relax and let those little memory jogs in the text point you to where the passing and cadence tones go. If you listen more than calculate, things will go better, for the reasons we saw in the last chapter.

Still, the evolution of the musical score with notes and staff lines is generally regarded as "progress" (it certainly was in my musicology classes). In terms of musical expression, written notation opens up two very significant options: it allows for a greater melodic complexity than can easily be handled by the ear alone, and it allows the music to be shared more widely. Mozart was legendary for being able to hear whole symphonies in his head, but most of us need to rely on a musical score when things get any more complex than the simple two-line couplets we practiced in the last chapter. Written notation opens up a whole wide world of psalmody.

As I mentioned in chapter 3, one of the happier outcomes of the Catholic Church's shelving of Gregorian chant in the wake of Vatican II is that it produced a contemporary revival of liturgical psalmody and a cornucopia of new psalm tones and mass settings. As the old Gregorian monolith collapsed, contemporary liturgical composers wrestled with the dual challenges of developing new vernacular settings for the former Latin texts, and creating a new musical language in which to notate them. The old Gregorian neumes had been a highly effective visual format once you'd learned to decipher them; what would take their place? Contemporary composers have been scrambling to develop appropriate and user-friendly new styles of notation that support the eye-ear connection while still conveying the melodic and rhythmic fluidity that are the essence of nonmensural chant.

As you might expect, a period of such radical experimentation and ferment is bound to produce a certain variation in approaches, and this can be disconcerting initially when you make the rounds of monastic communities and encounter what appear to be completely different notational systems. But beneath all the flux (and not counting the apparent quick fix of simply transcribing the new texts back into the old Gregorian neumes[1]), most contemporary psalmody adheres to one of three basic systems, or "schools," of notational thought, and we'll be exploring them all in this chapter. Once you recognize which system you're operating in, it's a lot easier to get oriented.

System One: Reciting Tone/Cadence Tone

Let's start with the most straightforward of these systems, which is essentially a natural extension of the Suzuki psalmody we've already been doing. For this first exercise in sight-singing, we'll be working with Psalm

100, the well-known "Shout to the Lord, all you lands," in a setting by the monks of New Camaldoli Monastery for Thursday lauds. Listen to the chant on track 10 of your CD as you follow the text below: [CD track 10]

Shout with joy to the Lord, all you / lands.
Serve the Lord \ with gladness.
Come into his presence \ rejoicing.

Know that the Lord is / God.
He made us and we \ are his,
his own people, the sheep of \ his pasture.

Come into his gates, giving / thanks.
Enter his courts \ with praise.
Give thanks to him and bless \ his name.

Praise the Lord, for he is / good,
his love endures \ for ever,
his faithfulness from age \ to age.

Praise the Father for his merciful / love;
taste and see that the Lord \ is good;
give him praise in the Ho \ ly Spirit.[2]

Now let's get oriented for sight-singing. At the top of the page, you'll see what looks like three musical measures. Underneath each one is a caption: "Odd lines," "Even lines," and "Last line only." These three "measures"[3] comprise the psalm tone we'll be using to sing the psalm.

Below the music, you'll see the text of this psalm set in a slightly curious way. Just before the end of the first line there is an upward slash mark (/) separating "Shout with joy to the Lord, all you" and "lands." That little slash is your important orientation point; it tells you how to match the text to the music. Everything to the left side of that slash is sung on the single white note on the pitch G. (For those of you who know how to read music, that white note looks like a dotted half note, but it isn't; in this context, the white note is simply the reciting tone.) The one remaining syllable on the right hand of the slash is sung on the remaining note, the black one—which looks like a quarter note in standard musical symbolism but is actually the cadence tone.

The second line of text matches the second measure of music in exactly the same way. Again, everything to the left side of the slash is sung on the reciting tone. After the slash, a note that looks like an eighth note (it has a little flag on its stem) presents itself as the passing tone and matches the syllable "with." The last two syllables of the line—the word *gladness*—are both sung on the final note of the measure, the cadence tone.

The third measure of the psalm tone—which, of course, matches the third line of the text—works exactly the same way. Everything to the left of the slash is sung on the reciting tone. On the right, the passing tone matches the syllable "to," while the cadence tone matches the syllables "joicing." (If you're alert, you may have noticed that an upward slash indicates that the next note to be sung will be a higher pitch than the one you're leaving; a downward slash—or backslash—indicates a lower pitch.)

There, you've done it! Now just continue this way through the twelve lines of the psalm and the three-line doxology, and you've sight-read your first psalm tone.

Why odd lines and even lines, you may wonder. Why not just first line, second line, and third line? The reason is perhaps not obvious in Psalm 100. But it becomes clear shortly when, toward the end of this same Thursday morning office, you arrive at the *Benedictus*, or Song of Zechariah (Luke 1:68–79), the traditional canticle appointed for monastic morning prayer.[4] Here we have the same basic notational system as before: three "measures," designated odd, even, and last line only:

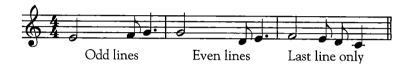

Odd lines   Even lines   Last line only

But when you start to match these "measures" with the text, you'll find yourself in a very different situation from before. Here's the text, with its slash marks:

> Blessed be the Lord, the God / of Israel:
> he has visited and ransomed \ his people.
> He has raised up for us a migh / ty Savior,
> born of the house of his \ servant David.
>
> He spoke through the mouths of / his holy ones,
> those who were his prophets in an \ cient times;
> he promised to free us from / our enemies
> and from the hands of \ all our foes.
>
> Toward our ancestors he was e / ver merciful,
> keeping in mind his ho \ ly covenant,
> the oath he had sworn to our fa / ther Abraham,
> that rid of fear and safe from \ the foe

we might serve him all the days of / our lives,
and stand in his presence, a just and \ holy
    people.

As for you, O child, you shall / be called
a prophet of the Most \ High God,
for you shall go ahead of / the Lord
to lay out straight paths \ before him,
that his people may know their / salvation
in the remission of \ all their sins.

Through the loving kindness of / our God
the Dayspring from on high \ shall visit us,
illumining those in darkness and shadowed /
    by death
and guiding our steps in the \ path of peace.

**Give thanks to the Most / High God,
who has raised up for us a migh \ ty Savior,
his own Son and Son / of David:
the Dayspring, Jesus \ Christ our Lord.**

As you can see, rather than the lockstep three lines per verse of Psalm
100, this canticle has variable-length verses, alternating between four and
six lines. The odd/even/last formula makes good sense here. The odd lines
(1, 3, and sometimes 5) are sung to the odd lines measure; the even ones
(2 and sometimes 4) are sung to the even lines measure; the last line of the
verse, whether odd or even, is sung to the last line measure. This provides
a simple way for the length of the verses to expand or contract, accommodating more fluid translations and a more graceful matching of the poetry
to the music. You can listen to this beautiful canticle on track 11 of your
CD. [CD track 11] ◉

System Two: Triple-Stress Pattern

The first system of notation is straightforward, and if it were the only game in town, you'd now be well on your way to mastering chant notation. But it isn't. Here's an alternative system that you'll also find is commonly used in monastic communities:

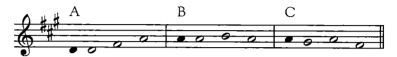

O sing a new sóng to the Lórd,
sing to the Lórd all the eárth.
O síng to the Lórd, bless his náme.

Proclaim his hélp day by dáy,
tell among the nátions his glóry
and his wónders among áll the peóples.

The Lord is great and wórthy of práise,
to be feared abóve all góds;
the góds of the héathens are náught.

It was the Lord who máde the heávens,
his are majesty and státe and pówer
and spléndor in his hóly place.

Give the Lord, you fámilies of peóples,
give the Lord glóry and pówer;
give the Lórd the glóry of his náme.

Bring an offering and énter his córurts,
worship the Lórd in his témple.
O eárth, trémble befóre him.

Proclaim to the nátions: "God is Kíng."
The world he made fírm in its pláce;
he will júdge the péoples in fáirness.

What's going on here? Obviously, there must be a different operating principle at work. If you're used to thinking that the white note is always the reciting tone, what are you going to do with three of them in one measure? What does the black note mean? If it's a passing or cadence tone, why does it come first?

To solve these mysteries, we need to learn a bit of recent history and formally introduce into our study the name Joseph Gelineau, one of the towering patriarchs of contemporary liturgical psalmody. A French Jesuit and one of that first great wave of scholar-poets who began the work of translating the Latin Vulgate into the vernacular during the 1950s, he headed up the team responsible for the French translation of the psalms in *La Bible de Jerusalem*. The Grail Psalms are an English translation of the French, and when you work with these psalms (as you're likely to in most contemporary monastic psalters), you encounter the hand of Gelineau. A composer as well as a scholar, he created the lion's share of those fluid, hauntingly expressive psalm tones you'll still find in wide use today, both in monasteries and parishes; they are the cornerstone of contemporary Catholic liturgical psalmody.[5]

The key to understanding Gelineau psalmody lies in remembering that his translations are based on the rhythmic pattern of the original Hebrew psalter. This pattern features a steady rhythmic pulse and a regular number of stressed syllables per line, together with an irregular number of unstressed syllables. You'll see this pattern clearly recreated in the Grail Psalms, where in most cases each versicle will tend to have three strong stress points—that is, three syllables that the voice will naturally emphasize. For example, in the Grail translation of Psalm 57:

Have **mercy** on me, **God**, have **mercy**
For in **you** my **soul** has taken **refuge**;
In the **shadow** of your **wings** I take **refuge**
Till the **storms** of destruc**tion** pass **by.**

Musically, Gelineau's psalm tones tend to favor these three accented points with a change in pitch; they became the basic "pivot points" of the melody. His psalm tones typically feature three strong notes per versicle aligned with the stressed syllables, along with a variable number of un-stressed passing tones.

Perhaps this makes sense for the psalm tone we looked at earlier. Tran-scribed into this triple-stress pattern, the first verse of Psalm 96 would go like this:

O **sing** a new **song** to the **Lord,**
Sing to the **Lord,** all the **earth.**
O **sing** to the **Lord,** bless his **name.**

This is exactly what you're seeing in the musical notation. The white notes represent the three stressed syllables in the line; they match up with the accents over the syllables in the text. (Typically, only the second and third are marked with an accent; the first you'll get by ear). The black notes represent unstressed syllables before (or between) the major stress points. Turn to track 12 on your CD to hear how this psalm tone sounds. [CD track 12] ⊙

Gelineau psalmody is quite satisfying to sing and lends itself naturally to contemplative expression. While not exactly mensural chant, the steady underlying pulse and three accented "beats" have a distinctly rhythmic quality, which I've discovered falls easily on the heartbeat and allows the psalms to become a work of the heart quickly and deeply.

A Minor Variation

While all Grail/Gelineau psalmody is based on this triple-stress line rhythm, not all of it is notated according to the three-note pattern we just encountered. Quite often you'll encounter Gelineau-type psalmody transcribed in the reciting tone/cadence tone format of System One. A typical example is Psalm 57 as it appears in the "old" Camaldolese Psalter:[6]

> Have mercy on me, God, have mércy,
> for in you my soul has táken réfuge.
> In the shadow of your wings I take réfuge
> till the storms of destruction páss by.
>
> I call to God the Móst Hígh,
> to God who has always béen my hélp.
> May he send from heaven and sáve me
> and shame those who assáil me.
> May God send his truth and his lóve.
>
> My soul lies down amóng líons
> who would devour us, óne and áll.
> Their teeth are spéars and árrows,
> their tongue a shárpened swórd.
> O God, arise above the heávens;
> may your glory shíne on eárth!

They laid a snare for my stéps,
my soul was bowed dówn.
They dug a pit in my páth,
but fell in it themsélves.

My heart is ready, O Gód,
my heart is réady.
I will sing, I will sing your práise.
Awake, my sóul,
awake, lyre and hárp,
I will awake the dáwn.

I will thank you, Lord, among the péoples,
among the nations I will práise you,
for your love reaches to the heávens
and your truth to the skíes.
O God, arise above the heávens;
may your glory shine on eárth!

Give praise to the Father almíghty,
to his son, Jesus Christ the lórd,
to the spirit who dwells in our heárts,
both now and forever, Amén.

Once you get the hang of it, the system is fairly easy to decipher. As before, the white note designates the reciting tone, while the three black notes are passing tones and the cadence tone. The matchup to the text is indicated by the two small dots for the passing tones and an accent mark for the cadence tone.

Hence, the first line, "Have mercy on me, God, have mercy," would look like this in modern music notation:

Have mercy on me,   God,   have   mer-cy.

What about the letters above the musical "measures"? These correspond to the individual lines of each stanza, and as you can see, we are
dealing once again with an expandable psalm tone. As in the system we
looked at earlier, provision is made to accommodate a variable verse
length. In this case, however, the middle "measures" (C and D) serve as
the expansion couplers, added in when the line is six lines long. When the
line is only four lines long, you sing A-B-E-F. (When it's five lines long, as
in verse 2, you sing A-B-C-D-F; these subtleties are not always sufficiently
notated in the Psalter, but you'll pick them up quickly by ear if you know
what to expect.) This basically creates "mix-and-match" melodies, each
with its own character and beauty.[7] Listen to this psalm on track 13 of your
CD. [CD track 13] ◉

System Three: Steady Pulse

The third notational system is visually a mirror image of the first one. In
System One, what looked like a measure equated to a line of text. In System Three, a measure equates to an individual note in the psalm tone. All
the words sung on this note are written beneath it in the score. When the
note changes, a bar line (or new measure) marks the shift.

On page 109 is a Gelineau psalm tone, in this case for Psalm 51, transcribed in this format:[8] You can listen to it on track 14 of your CD. [CD
track 14] ◉

From what you've already learned in System Two, you'll be able to
make sense of this tone fairly easily. The "whole notes" arrange themselves
into that same underlying pattern of three stressed syllables per line:

Have **mercy** on me, **God** in your **kindness,**
In your compassion **blot** out my **offense.**
O **wash** me more and **more** from my **guilt**
And **cleanse** me **from** my **sin.**

The black notes again represent the unstressed pickup notes before the next stressed syllable.

This system has become increasingly favored in contemporary liturgical psalmody because of its ability to indicate subtle innuendos of pulse and tempo that are difficult to convey in the other two systems. The key to getting comfortable with this format lies in realizing that these "measures" really represent a basic pulse that remains steady throughout the chant: one slow pulse per "measure." The intervening unstressed syllables fall at the rate and flow of natural speech—a wonderful way of combining the the mensural and nonmensural worlds.

The best way to get used to sight-reading in this notational format is to start with the text alone. Tap your foot (or use a metronome) to establish a basic pulse; then practice fitting the words to the measure in which they belong so that they flow easily and naturally. This approach will also get you around what I find to be the biggest visual challenge with this form of notation: the tendency of the mind to think that a measure with a lot of words in it needs to be rushed. This is simply a visual miscue. It doesn't. The pulse remains the same: slow, easy, steady, one pulse per "measure." If you trust the pulse and practice relaxing into it, you'll see the syllables fit themselves in when and where they belong without strain or forcing. Once you're comfortable with the text, practice the psalm tone alone a few times, humming or using a neutral syllable so that you imprint it in your ear as a melody. Then you'll find that the tune and the words flow together nearly effortlessly.

1. Have   mercy on me, God, in your kindness.
2. My of - fenses   truly I   know them;
3. A   pure heart cre - ate for me, O God,
4. Give me a - gain the joy of your help;

1. In your com - passion blot out my of - fense.
2.   my   sin is   always be - fore me.
3.   put a   steadfast   spirit with - in me.
4.   with a   spirit of   fervor sus - tain me.

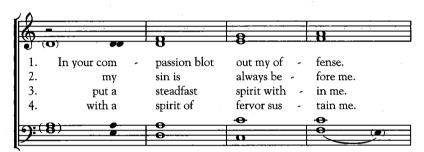

1.   O   wash me more and more from my guilt
2. Against you, you a - lone, have I sinned;
3. Do not cast me a - way from your presence,
4.   O   Lord, _____ open my   lips

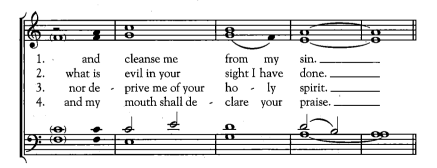

1.   and   cleanse me   from my   sin. _____
2. what is evil in your sight I have done. _____
3. nor de - prive me of your ho - ly   spirit. _____
4. and my mouth shall de - clare your praise. _____

As you've experienced for yourself at this point, modern liturgical and monastic psalmody is a young art that's still somewhat in flux. Nearly fifty years after Vatican II, stable patterns are gradually beginning to emerge. But as with Heisenberg's uncertainty principle, how these broad patterns will affect any given particle (you) at any given location (the monastic community with whom you're chanting) is not completely predictable. In a basic text such as this, I can't begin to cover all the exceptions, variations, and stylistic quirks (not to mention plain old transcription errors) that you'll find in individual house psalters that are still hand-cut and pasted together from a variety of sources and composers. But with these three basic systems under your belt, you ought to be able to follow along and join confidently in this beautiful ancient art form being born anew.

 10

The WIDE WORLD *of* ANTIPHONS

AS WE CONTINUE our tour of monastic psalmody, I should add one other fact about the monastic way of singing psalms. Generally speaking, the psalms for the Divine Office tend to come packaged in the form of "psalm sandwiches." If you can imagine the psalm as the meat of this sandwich, the bread on either side is provided by a contrasting musical composition known as an *antiphon*.[1] As in any good sandwich, the purpose of the bread is to help you get your hands around the contents, while at the same time highlighting the flavor.

Musically, the antiphon is a contrasting melodic line, usually a bit more tuneful than the psalm tone itself. The closest equivalent is a "refrain," and like all good refrains, an effective antiphon will stick in your mind easily and keep singing itself inside you long after the psalm itself is over. Down at the pump house, when the old water pump I'd been struggling to repair finally groaned back to life and I spontaneously burst into "With joy you will draw water from the fountain of salvation," it was an antiphon I was singing—in this case, the "bread" around the canticle from Isaiah from vigils that morning. It was obviously doing its job well.

But while a refrain is an integral part of the song both musically and textually, an antiphon is definitely an independent composition. The psalm can stand on its own without any antiphon at all, or it can be decked out in a variety of different antiphons to complement the liturgical season or commemorate a specific feast day. The text for the antiphon is typically drawn from a line in the psalm itself, but it can also come from a different part of the Old Testament, from the New Testament, or on rare occasions from a nonscriptural source. Wherever it comes from, its major functions are to reinforce the message of the psalm and to set the psalm in context either liturgically or theologically.

As an example of a basic psalm/antiphon combination, here's Psalm 63 from the New Camaldoli Psalter, together with its usual antiphon. You can listen to it on track 15 of your CD. [CD track 15] ⊙

In the sha-dow of your wings   I   re-joice, al - le - lu - ia!

Odd lines   Even lines   Last line only

O God, my God, at dawn / I seek you,
For you my soul is thirsting, my flesh / is longing,
Like a dry and parched land longs \ for water.

I have gazed on you in / the holy place,
To behold your might and / your glory.
Better than life itself is / your love.
My lips will sing \ your praise.

So I shall bless you all my / life long,
Lifting up my hands to invoke / your name;

My soul will be filled as with / rich feasting,
And my mouth will proclaim \ your praise.

I remember you as I lie on / my bed,
On you I meditate through the watches of / the night.
For you, O God, have come \ to aid me.

I rejoice in the shadow of / your wings,
To you my soul has / held fast,
You have sustained me by your \ right hand.

As you can see, the text for the antiphon ("In the shadow of your wings I rejoice, alleluia!") is drawn from the fifth verse of the psalm. A beautiful metaphor in its own right, it condenses the entire meaning of the psalm into a vivid musical "pith saying."

From this example, we can also see something about the musical aspects of antiphon/psalm tone coupling. Your ear alone will tell you that the psalm and its antiphon sandwich match somehow; they seem to be in the same "key." To be a bit more technical, they are actually in the same mode (remember our discussion of plainsong modes in chapter 8). In this case, we are in mode 1, and the plaintive, minor melody of the psalm tone is carried through in the antiphon. Just as most people would turn up their noses at a spicy, Genoa salami sandwich served on raisin bread, an antiphon wants to be of a compatible musical texture and "taste" to its host psalm. Often the melodic line of the antiphon will mirror the general musical shape of the psalm tone and begin and end either on the same note as the psalm tone or on a compatible harmonic interval, almost always the fifth.

A Practical Note

Remember when you're singing with the monastic choir that a sandwich requires *two* pieces of bread! You sing the antiphon first, then all the verses of the psalm, including the doxology, then the antiphon again. This instruction will not necessarily be written in your psalmbook. I can't tell the number of times I've been caught out, flipping ahead to the next psalm in the Divine Office without remembering to go back for the reprise of the antiphon.

The order is as follows:

1. Antiphon
2. Psalm (to psalm tone)
3. Doxology (to psalm tone)
4. Antiphon

Occasionally, when the psalmody is short and simple, you'll encounter the practice of singing the antiphon, then all the psalms for the day (usually there are only two of them, sung on the same psalm tone), then the antiphon again. It's the same sandwich principle, but in a more compressed format.

An Antiphon for All Seasons

The antiphons will generally vary with the seasons of the church year. During the Easter season, for example, if you were to join the monks of New Camaldoli for lauds, you'd hear our old friend Psalm 100 ("Shout with joy to the Lord, all you lands") decked out in the following antiphon:

You can listen to the combination on track 16 of your CD. [CD track 16] ⊚ The text for this antiphon comes from Matthew 28:7, a section of the Easter Gospel. These are the words Jesus spoke to the faithful women who held vigil at the tomb and became the first witnesses to his resurrection. The antiphon provides a moving and effective way of tying the psalm to the liturgical theme of the day: "Shout with joy to the Lord, all you lands" is now set within the context of the Easter resurrection message. That's the artistry of monastic psalmody.

Now let's imagine that you were to return to New Camaldoli for the week following Christmas. Again, you'd encounter Psalm 100, but this time clothed in the following antiphon, as heard on track 17 of your CD: [CD track 17] ⊚

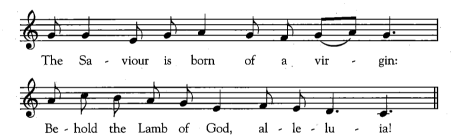

The Sa - viour is born of a vir - gin:

Be - hold the Lamb of God, al - le - lu - ia!

From this one example, you can grasp the basic principle of monastic psalmody. The principle is always the same, whether it's the mystical Latin of Gregorian chant or the plain English of contemporary psalmody. With variable antiphons around the fixed psalm tone (the "meat" of the psalm sandwich), a subtle cross-referencing is always going on: to the liturgical season (the time of the church year in which the psalm is being sung), to other bits of scriptural texts, or to the interplay between Old and New Testament. For better or worse, there is always a subtle contextualization at work in monastic psalmody, an intimation that the yearnings expressed in the psalms find their fulfillment in Christ.

If you are so attuned, you can tell instantly where you are in the liturgical year simply by the psalmody. Each season has its own color, its own textual and musical ambience created by the mode of the psalm tones and the text and musical quality of the antiphons. They match as closely and vividly as the vestments and altar frontals—red, green, purple, white—to mark the changing seasons of the Christian year. I could be blindfolded and dropped from outer space into the chapel at New Camaldoli, and as soon as I heard the cantor launch into "Be not afraid; go tell my friends to set out for Galilee," I'd know instantly that we were at lauds during the season of Easter.

Indeed, much of the wealth and sensuous beauty of the Christian liturgy is drawn from its rich treasury of antiphons. The haunting *"Puer Natus"* from the famous *Chant* album by the monks of Santo Domingo de Silos (the one that astounded everyone by making it to the top of the pop charts a few years back) proves to be—once you pare it down to bare essentials—"merely" a classic psalm with antiphon. The meat of this psalm sandwich is Psalm 98: "Sing to the Lord a new song." The antiphon *"Puer natus nobis"* is the well-loved Christmas text (from Isaiah, and of Handel's *Messiah* fame): "For unto us a child is born, unto us a son is given." Those listeners who knew their way around monastic psalmody (and the Latin language) would have suspected, even without reading the liner notes, that what they were hearing was part of the monastic psalmody for Christmas day. It's like knowing a secret language that adds depth and subtlety to the overt proclamation of scripture.

The Creative Edge

In medieval times, antiphonaries—that is, collections of antiphons—were always far more numerous than any other type of liturgical manuscript, and it's not hard to see why. Each psalm in regular use during the Divine Office would require a trousseau of antiphons for the six major liturgical seasons of the church year (Advent, Christmas, Epiphany, Lent,

Eastertide, and Pentecost), plus several more for specific feast days—in other words, nearly one thusand mix-and-match tunes right then and there. Add to that the additional variable of antiphons to match the eight plainsong modes (meaning several different musical settings of the same text), and you can see how the numbers begin to increase geometrically. And that's even before we get to the most interesting feature of the antiphons, their creativity.

Almost since the start, the antiphons have offered fertile ground for the religious imagination. Nothing seems to satisfy quite so much as coming up with a striking new combination—the "Easter Gospel" antiphons at New Camaldoli, as a case in point—or a tuneful new setting of an old text, or finding a line or phrase lurking inconspicuously within the psalm that suddenly throws a whole new ray of light on its meaning. If liturgy is always to some degree composed of fixed and variable parts, the antiphons have classically been a growing edge: Sometimes, like all fast-growing vines, they need pruning, but they are the place where the life force of the now and the individual most keenly dialogues with the traditional and the unchanging. This is an important point, to which we'll return at the end of this chapter.

The O Antiphons

Among the most beautiful and justly famous examples of antiphon creativity are the "O Antiphons," which for well over a thousand years of Christian practice have been sung during the week immediately preceding Christmas (December 17 through 23). They are a matched set of seven antiphons to be sung as the bread around the meat of the *Magnificat*, the canticle for vespers.

They're called the O Antiphons because they all start with the invocation "O. . . ." In fact, you've probably encountered them whether you know it or not, because they furnish the text for the seven verses of the familiar advent hymn "O Come, O Come, Emmanuel":

O come, thou Wisdom from on high, who orders
all things mightily;
To us the path of knowledge show, and teach us
in her ways to go. . . . [*refrain*]

O come, O come, thou Lord of might, who to thy
tribes on Sinai's height
In ancient times did give the law, in cloud and
majesty and awe. . . . [*refrain*]

O come, thou rod of Jesse's stem, from every foe
deliver them
That trust thy mighty power to save, and give
them victory o'er the grave. . . . [*refrain*]

O come, thou key of David, come, and open wide
our heavenly home;
Make safe the way that leads on high, and close
the path to misery. . . . [*refrain*]

O come, thou Dayspring from on high, and cheer
us by thy drawing nigh;
Disperse the gloomy clouds of night, and death's
dark shadow put to flight. . . . [*refrain*]

O come, desire of nations, bind in one the heart
of all humankind;
Bid thou our sad divisions cease, and be thyself
our King of Peace. . . . [*refrain*]

O come, O come, Emmanuel, and ransom captive
   Israel
That mourns in lonely exile here until the Son of
   God appear. . . . [refrain]

[refrain: Rejoice, rejoice! Emmanuel shall come
   to thee, O Israel!]

Rather than forming one endlessly long hymn, in the monastic rendition, you'll hear each of these O invocations separately—one per day—as they interweave themselves around the ancient and beautiful words of Mary's song of praise in her response to the Annunciation. One of the simplest and most effective settings is in use at Saint Benedict's Monastery; I'll quote it here in full to give you a sense of how antiphon and canticle fit together and to give you a no-frills version you can chant yourself if you feel moved to incorporate this traditional Christian practice into your own spiritual preparation for Advent.[2] You'll find it on track 18 of your CD. [CD track 18]

DECEMBER 17

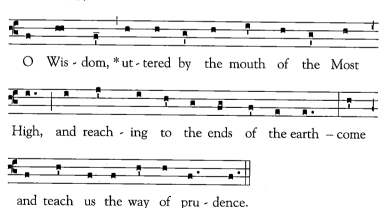

O Wis - dom, * ut - tered by the mouth of the Most

High, and reach - ing to the ends of the earth – come

and teach us the way of pru - dence.

DECEMBER 18

O A-do-na-i, * rul-er of the house of Is-ra-el,

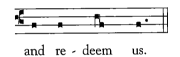

who ap-peared to Mo-ses in the burn-ning bush — come

and re-deem us.

DECEMBER 19

O Root of Jes-se, * Stan-dard of the na-tions and

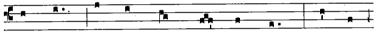

of kings; whom the whole world im-plores — come and

de-li-ver us.

DECEMBER 20

O Key of Dav-id * and Scep-tre of the house of Is-ra -

el, what you op - en none can shut – come and lead

us out of dark - ness.

DECEMBER 21 (SOLSTICE)

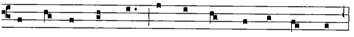

O Ra - diant Dawn, *splen-dor of e - ter-nal light

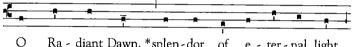

and Sun of jus - tice, shine on those lost in dark - ness

– come to en-light-en us.

DECEMBER 22

O King of the na - tions, * so long de - sired, cor - ner -

stone un - it - ing hu - man - kind – come and save the

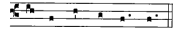

work of your cre - a - tion.

O Em-ma-nu-el, * God pre-sent in our midst, long

a-wait-ed Sa-vior and King — come and save us, O

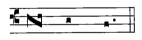

Lord our God.

MAGNIFICAT PSALM TONE

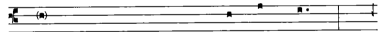

My soul proclaims the greatness of the Lórd,

My spirit rejoices in God my sáv-ior;

For he has looked with favor on his low-lỹ
    sér-vant,
and from this day all generations will call
    mĕ bléss-ed.

The Almighty has done great things fôr mé:
    holy is hǐs náme.

He has mercy on those whô feár him
    in every gen-ĕr-á-tion.

Repeat O Antiphon

He has shown the strength of hîs árm,
he has scattered the proud in thĕir cónceit.

He has cast down the mighty from thêir thrónes,
and has lifted up thĕ lów-ly.

He has filled the hungry with goôd thíngs,
and sent the rich away emp-tў́ hánd-ed.

He has come to the help of his servant Is-râ-él,
for he remembered his pro-mĭse óf mer-cy.

Repeat O Antiphon

The promise he made to oûr fá-thers,
to Abraham and his childrĕn for év-er.

Glory to the Father, and to thê Són,
 and to the Ho-lў́ Spí-rit.

As in the bê-gín-ning,
so now and for ev-ĕr. Á-men.

Repeat O Antiphon

As you ponder the powerful, archetypal imagery at work here, you'll glimpse something of the creative genius of antiphons. Through these seven successive invocations, the birth of Christ is reflected through the lens of holy Wisdom and universal peace; the context is cosmic, sophianic, feminine, and inclusive. Even though these words are among the most ancient in the liturgy (I remember working with them in an eighth-century Old English translation when I was a graduate student), they are still profoundly, mystically contemporary. My heart quivers each year as I gather myself once again to pray them; it's like renewing my vows as a Christian for the upcoming year, recommitting myself to what is deepest and most universal on my own spiritual path. Through their poetry and fluidity, antiphons can soften the hard edges of dogma and theology and create a more spacious home for the soul, reverberating with that which does, in fact, "bind in one the hearts of all humankind."

Is Christ the Fulfillment of Scripture?

I deliberately intoduced the O Antiphons before addressing an important piece of unfinished business from a sentence I wrote a few pages back: For better or worse, there is always a subtle contextualization at work in monastic psalmody, an intimation that the yearnings expressed in the psalms find their fulfillment in Christ.

Did this statement make you uneasy? If it did, you're rightfully sensitive to what, along with the violence in the psalmody, is unquestionably the deepest conundrum for Christian practice built on an Old Testament foundation. For twenty centuries of Christian self-understanding, it was essentially a foregone conclusion that Christ was the "fulfillment of scripture," Israel's long-awaited Messiah, and all the currents in the Church's theology and liturgy set in that direction. Only in recent decades—spurred in large part by remorse for the Holocaust—has Christian conscience (by no means unanimously) begun to own its complicity in the tragedy through a teaching which for two thousand years has consistently devalued the rights of another faith tradition. That realization, in turn, has raised thorny questions about how best to untangle this Gordian knot.

The obvious starting point would seem to be a thorough liturgical housecleaning, and much of this work is well underway. In the Episcopal Church, for example, the Nicene Creed has now been amended to read "Christ rose *in accordance* with the scriptures (rather than *in fulfillment*), and almost universally, the traditional "imprecations" (or curses against the Jewish people) of the Good Friday liturgy have been rewritten as petitions for universal forgiveness and peace. All of this is a step in the right direction, toward forbearance. But this newfound sensibility soon finds itself swimming upstream against a powerful current of Christian tradition, not only theologically but in terms of spiritual practice. As we saw in chapter 5, the traditional training of the unitive imagination in lectio divina has hinged on the awakening of the second, or "christological," sense of scripture, in which all things are seen through the lens of Christ; and the antiphons have traditionally served as a prime ground for this training. The issues are not as simple as they appear, and they have profound implications for Christian spiritual practice.

There are those who would favor a radical pruning and revising of texts, so as to cover up or at least minimize the impact of this so-called supercessionist slant of Christian theology. Psalms would be sung with no antiphons or doxologies, allowing their essential Jewishness to stand. But this begs the real question, and it also leaves the liturgy cut off from one of its strongest internal resources for self-correction. My own preferred resolution is not *no* antiphons, but *new* antiphons.

By way of introduction—and as in the case of the violence of the psalms—it's useful to make a distinction between the spheres of public proclamation and contemplative practice. It's quite true that statements like "Christ is the fulfillment of all scripture" or "The New Testament supercedes the Old," when made from the pulpit and mirrored in the liturgy, can reinforce religious arrogance and intolerance. But in more than thirty years of intimate association with Christian contemplative monasticism, I can honestly say that I have yet to see a single example of the kind of rigid intolerance and literalism so typical of religious fundamentalism— and the reason, I'm convinced, lies in the practice of lectio divina itself. That narrow, either-or slant which has such a field day with statements such as John 14:11 ("I am the way, the truth, and the life; no one comes to the Father except through me") is characteristic of the first, or literal, sense of scripture (see chapter 5 to refresh your memory on this), and it is the whole business of monastic lectio to break down this sense and move the lens of perception steadily toward the unitive. At this final and deepest level, the supercessionist slant of Christian self-understanding takes on a whole new meaning. Rather than a proclamation of religious superiority, it is an affirmation of ultimate coherence: a realization that "in Christ all things hold together" (Colossians 1:17). Jesus is seen as the manifestation, in a particularly intense and luminous way, of the divine intelligence and mercy that undergird all created existence. Far from being exclusive, it is as inclusive and cosmic a statement as can be made.[3]

Which brings us back to the subject of antiphons. As we have seen, the antiphons are the most fluid and creative part of the liturgy, and their function has always been to invite a dialogue between what is fixed and unchanging (such as the ancient words of the psalms themselves) and the evolving perceptions and sensibilities of our own time. The solution to our present impasse is not to shelve the Church's rich treasury of antiphons, but simply to harness the creative power of the antiphon principle itself. If, as Ewert Cousins intimates in *Christ of the 21st Century*, human consciousness is headed toward a "second axial" period, in which unitive awareness becomes the "coin of the realm," then what's needed are antiphons that speak this new language.[4] Taking their place among the Church's vast repertory of antiphons, they will inevitably modify the impact of past understandings through the sheer weight of their presence.

We have seen how the O Antiphons, which are more than a thousand years old, still timelessly and beautifully set the birth of Christ within the Wisdom of eternal peace. The source of that Wisdom is still available to us. What would it be like, I wonder, to develop antiphons—whole new "trousseaus" of them—drawn from the poetry of Rumi or from the beautiful teachings of the Dalai Lama; Martin Luther King, Jr.; Etty Hillesum; Black Elk; or the Beatitudes? In this way, the psalms might be set free from the religious intransigence of an earlier era and reclaimed as the meat in a psalm sandwich whose bread is universal compassion and forgiveness.

Liturgical psalmody at its best has always been a rich confluence of word, music, and spiritual intuition. The way to incorporate the growing spiritual consciousness of our times is not to destroy the vehicle, but to liberate the creative principle at work in it, so that we can once again fashion "an intersection of the timeless with time" (in the words of the poet T. S. Eliot) that is appropriate to our own highest self-awareness. If the psalms have sometimes appeared to be swords, through their antiphons they can be beaten into plowshares.

11

READING
GREGORIAN
NOTATION

FOR NEARLY FORTY YEARS NOW, ever since that fateful decision of Vatican II to shelve Gregorian chant in favor of simpler, vernacular settings, contemplative psalmody has been in the midst of a minor renaissance. Along with crisp, singable new psalm settings have come simpler, less fussy ways of notating them. In chapter 9, we familiarized ourselves with some of the most popular styles of modern notation.

But every so often when you visit a monastery, you'll encounter music that's still written in Gregorian notation. The earliest monastic strategy for venturing into the vernacular was simply to write the new English texts using the old Gregorian neumes, and these early hybrids are still in common use, particularly when it comes to hymns or special music for feast days. At first, the notation may throw you for a loop, but once you've learned the basic characters in the Gregorian "alphabet," it's not terribly difficult to follow what's going on. In fact, many people find that it's actually easier than modern notation.

Let's learn a few of these basics with a simple alleluia chant. This joyous little chant is sung every year at Saint Benedict's Monastery as an antiphon for the psalmody in the week immediately following Easter. Eastertide (the fifty days from Easter to Pentecost) is a church season when alleluias peal forth everywhere, and this tiny little chant contains eight of them! Here's what it looks like on the printed page:

Al - le - lu - ia, al - le - lu - ia, al - le - lu - ia, al - le -

lu - ia, al - le - lu - ia, al - le - lu - ia, al - le - lu - ia, al - le - lu - ia.

The first thing you may notice is that the Gregorian staff, unlike modern notation, has only four lines. The key to orienting yourself is that little symbol that looks like a telephone receiver on the third line up. It's called a clef sign, and it tells you that middle C, as we'd call it in modern sight-reading (or more correctly "do," as in do-re-mi) is on the third line. So the first of those eight alleluias, transcribed into modern notation, would look like this:

Al - le - lu - ia

The single, square notes of the Gregorian notation are the basic pulse of this chant. Each one is called a *punctum*.[1] Most modern notation would render them as quarter notes or eighth notes. They can be sung at whatever tempo you want.

On the "lu" syllable, we encounter our first compound neume, or ligature, which simply means notes joined together. In this case, our neume is a *podatus*, which indicates that you read the notes from the bottom up:

lu -

On the second alleluia, we meet our second compound neume, which looks like a little hat. It's called a *torculus* and is used when the second in a group of three notes is higher than the others. You read it from left to right:

lu - ia ____

In the fourth alleluia, we meet another neume, known as a *clivis*. It's used to indicate decending notes (the opposite of a *podatus*). Again, you read it from left to right:

lu -

Thus, the entire antiphon, in modern notation, would read as follows (you can listen to it on track 19 of your CD): [CD track 19] ◉

Al-le-lu - ia, al-le-lu - ia, ____ al-le-lu-ia, al-le-lu - ia,

al-le-lu-ia, al-le-lu - ia, al-le - lu-ia, al - le - lu - ia.

One other minor point. The dot after the "ia" of *alleluia* means that this note is held longer. Custom varies here, but typically the note doubles in length.

This no-frills but lovely little alleluia serves well as an introduction to the rich heritage of Gregorian chanting. We've learned four of the ten basic characters in the Gregorian alphabet and had a chance to see how easily and naturally this alphabet flows in the eye-ear connection. The next chant we consider will fill in a few more pieces of the puzzle.

Reading More Complex Neumes

Let's use this *Kyrie Eleison* chant, also from the Easter season, to introduce some of the more complex three-, four-, and five-note neumes. The Kyrie is one of the chants for the Mass; the words (which are in Greek, not Latin) say, "Lord have mercy on us, Christ have mercy on us; Lord have mercy on us." This particular Kyrie is known as the *Kyrie Lux et origo* ("Light and Origin") a sumptuously mystical image for the Easter season. You'll find it in the *Liber Usualis*; you can also listen to it on track 20 of your CD: [CD track 20]

Again, as we orient ourselves on the four-line Gregorian staff, we find that small "telephone receiver" indicating that middle C (or "do") is on the third line. Occasionally in Gregorian notation, you'll also meet up with a variant clef sign that looks like this:

It indicates that the fourth note of the scale (or "fa") is on the indicated line.

The first Kyrie is essentially familiar territory from our first lesson with the alleluia. In modern notation, it would look like this:

Ky - ri - e _____ e - le - i - son

The small, diamond-shaped notes have exactly the same time value as the square *puncta*. They are typically used for notes that descend stepwise. With further regard to the time value of notes, it is probably best to repeat verbatim the instructions from the *Liber Usualis*: "Each note in Plainsong, whether isolated or in a group, whatever be its shape, has the same value, the value of a quaver [eighth note] in figured music."[2]

One other important point to keep in mind is that repeated notes on the same pitch sung on the same syllables are interpreted as being tied together—hence, double in time value. I've marked the first time this formation occurs with an asterisk; you'll meet it several other times in this Kyrie.

In the Christe section, we meet up with a succession of three-note neumes. Their official names are *torculus* and *porrectus*, respectively (we've already met the torculus in our first lesson; it's the little hat-shaped neume). In the *porrectus*, which looks sort of like a flag, the first pitch is located on the space, the second on the lower line, and the third on the upper line. The *porrectus* is used when the second note in the group is lower than the other two. Here's how the sequence would look in modern notation:

To complete our tour of the three-note neumes, we should add the third, called a *scandicus*. It's the last of our basic repertory of neumes, used when the line is ascending:

Over the syllable "Chri" in the *Christe*, you'll notice a horizontal line. It's known as an *episema* and indicates a slight lengthening of the time value of the note; it's not strictly mathematical, but more a matter of gesture and innuendo.

As we move into the *eleison* in this section, we find our first six-note group. But what may at first seem like complexity disentangles to a simple two-note podatus—which you read from the bottom up—followed by a stepwise descending line:

The third Kyrie is then sung as follows:

Ky - ri - e _____ e - le - i - son

And the final one like this:

Ky-ri - e _____ e - le - i - son

If you're wondering about that little hieroglyphic *iij* after the Kyrie
and Christe sections, this instructs you to sing each of these sections three
times. The next-to-last Kyrie has *ij*—which means you sing it twice—and
the last Kyrie is sung only once. Altogether, you've sung three Kyries,
three Christes, and three more Kyries. This "ninefold Kyrie" is standard
practice in Gregorian chant and is still observed in most monasteries
today.

Expanding Your Knowledge

These two basic lessons are enough to get you up and running in Gregorian chanting. Of course, it goes without saying that we've only scratched
the surface. Like an iceberg, nine-tenths of the art is below the waterline.
The fine points, which the monks of Solesmes made a lifetime's work,
don't have as much to do with reading the neumes as with subtle gestures
of inflection, lengthening of notes, and accentuation. There are more
complicated neumes, variations of the basic alphabet we've learned, that
provide for these subtleties. *Liquescents*, smaller-sized notes within a com-

pound neume, indicate that smaller note is to be sung more lightly, as does the *quilisma*, a jagged note that looks something like a lightning bolt running through the neume in question. In the case of the quilisma, however, the note immediately preceding it is "notably lengthened," according to the *Liber Usualis*—once again, more by feel than by strict formula.[3] These subtleties are what constitute the real high art of Gregorian chanting. If you can possibly lay your hands on a *Liber Usualis*, by all means do so; you'll find these and many more fine points of this rarified art form meticulously explained and illustrated.

Perhaps as you've worked with the neumes, you've found it easier to read the old neumes than their modern equivalents. There is a reason for this, again an aspect of that conscious art I referred to in chapter 3. Half calligraphy, the Gregorian neumes beautifully express the liquidity of the Latin chant and subliminally direct you how to sing it; I've always been surprised how those descending diamonds send you the subliminal eye message to "lighten up" on a descending line, which is essential to maintaining pitch and fluidity. It's a perfect case of medium and message. The chant in modern notation always seems too pointillistic, one note too isolated from the next. Once you get used to the Gregorian neumes, you'll find that you can follow along amazingly well.

One final point when singing Gregorian chant: remember that this is a learned oral tradition. The basic operations can be learned from a book, but there are subtleties in blend, pacing, and holding and energizing notes that are worked out in long hours in the monastic choir and become part of the common life of the community. What invariably causes distress to monks is cocky visitors who, having learned their chant in a conservatory setting, go blasting through like an eighteen-wheeler, completely lost in their own competence. One of the reasons Gregorian chant does not easily transplant beyond the walls of the monastery is that the tempering and melding are arrived at from deep within, from the life itself. No matter how impressive the vocal pyrotechnics, Gregorian chant sung by a profes-

12

CUSTOMIZING YOUR PSALMODY

A S THE LAST FEW CHAPTERS HAVE DEMONSTRATED, the contemporary revival of contemplative chanting and psalmody has created an abundant supply of new psalm settings from which to pick and choose. But what if you live in a part of the country where music materials are not easily available? Or what if you're uncertain of your sight-reading skills and a bit intimidated by the prospect of singing from a score? Or what if nothing you find quite matches the tunes singing themselves in your head or the translations you want to use? There's a simple and time-honored solution to all these problems. Why not try your hand at composing?

Developing your own psalm settings and antiphons is not really difficult and gives you a tremendous freedom to sing the psalms to whatever melodies you like. Even more important, it carries your psalmody to a whole new level of engagement. The fifth-century Desert Father John Cassian once observed that he knew monks had reached the unitive sense of scripture (the highest level of spiritual understanding) when "they sang the psalms as if they were composing them." The actual process of composing, bringing your own creative processes into play, unfolds newfound depths in the psalm-singing experience and makes the psalms even more your own prayer. In this chapter, we'll be looking at specific ways to do this.

Developing Your Own Psalm Tones

We actually began composing psalm tones in our very first lesson in psalm singing back in chapter 8, with the simple step-up, step-down tunes that can be sung completely by ear. You can return to track 3 on your CD to refresh your memory on our first psalm tone. Here's how it begins:

>I will bless the Lord at all **times;*** (step up)
>his praise shall ever be in my **mouth.** (step down)

In musical notation, the melody would look like this:

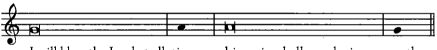

I will bless the Lord at all times,   his praise shall ever be in my mouth.

As I mentioned, this simple psalm tone will do the job for most two-line, or couplet, psalm formats, but in a rather singsong way. Once you're comfortable with the basic principle of pointing—that is, matching the steps up and the steps down of the psalm tone to the appropriate places in the text—I recommend moving on to the following simple and dignified melody, which will work for virtually any two-line psalm verses. As I mentioned earlier in the book, I sometimes call it the "Anglican tone" because it captures the flavor and spirit of the Anglican tradition of liturgical psalmody so well. Return to track 7 on your CD to hear how it goes.

If the two-line psalm you're working with occasionally expands to three lines, the standard way of dealing with the situation is to add an "expander" line on a single tone (or alternatively, a descending third for the cadence tone). The line to be expanded is usually marked with a dash at the end. Here's an example, using the first verse of Psalm 142:

> With all my voice I cry to the Lord—
> With all my voice I entreat the / Lord.
> I pour out my trou\ble before him.

You would sing this verse as follows:

With all my voice I cry to the Lord,

With all my voice I entreat the Lord.

I pour out my trou - ble   be-fore him.

(ALTERNATE FIRST LINE [DESCENDING THIRD])

With all my voice I cry to the Lord,

Turn to track 21 on your CD to hear how the two variations sound. [CD track 21] ◉

Over the years I have gradually accumulated a notebook of flexible, personally pleasing psalm tones in both major and minor modes that are suitable to adaptation for psalm verses of two, three, and four lines. This notebook furnishes my "basic wardrobe" of psalm tones, which I draw on to develop my repertoire of psalm settings. Whenever I find a psalm tone that I particularly like or that seems to fill a niche in terms of its tone color or basic versatility, I copy it into my notebook. It's exactly the same as developing your basic clothing wardrobe; you add items you like one piece at a time.

The psalm tones in the New Camaldoli Psalter, with their "odd lines/even lines/last line only" formula, are particularly useful because they can expand and contract to accommodate verses with an irregular number of lines. This beautiful little melody, used by the Camaldolese monks for many of their *Magnificat* and *Benedictus* settings, has a luminous, major mode feeling to it. You can hear it sung on track 22 of your CD. [CD track 22] ◉

Odd lines   Even lines   Last line only

As you develop your basic wardrobe of psalm tones, this is another Camaldolese melody (found on track 23 of your CD) with a more minor feel to it: [CD track 23] ◉

Odd lines   Even lines   Last line only

While this is "officially" the psalm tone for Psalm 63, you'll find it will work for any psalm with a three-line or longer verse length and a somewhat serious modality. Here I've adapted it to Psalm 57, and it is sung on track 24 of your CD. [CD track 24] ◉

> Have mercy on me, Lord, / have mercy,
> for in you my soul has ta / ken refuge,
> In the shadow of your wings I / take refuge
> till the storms of destruction \ pass by

You can listen to track 13 on your CD to compare the psalm in this setting with the version we looked at in chapter 9.

As you're developing your notebook of basic psalm tones, don't forget to include a few that will provide specifically for verses of four, five, and six lines. Here are a major and minor pair in present or former use at New Camaldoli, that are outstanding for their versatility as well as their beauty. You can hear them on tracks 25 and 26, respectively, of your CD. [CD tracks 25 and 26] ◉ The brackets around the middle letters indicate the measures that are eliminated when the verse is only four lines long.[1]

You can even compose your own original tunes. Melodies exist in virtually limitless combinations, limited only by the power of your imagination. Here's a simple expandable psalm tone I wrote myself, following the New Camaldoli model. You can find it on track 27 of your CD. [CD track 27]

Those of you who can read music will see that the basic pattern I followed was simply to develop the possibilities of a C-major chord. The first (odd-line) phrase is a simple tonic chord (so-mi-do), with "so" as the reciting tone. The second (even) line moves the reciting tone up one step—to "la"—a familiar musical pattern. The next odd line drops the reciting tone back to "so" again, while the last-line-only cadence formula goes straight down the scale from there and ends on "do": the key in which this little tone is sung.

What if you don't read or write music? Your ear is the composer, not your mind. After all, you've been listening to music since you were a baby, and even if you don't know the technical terms, the patterns are still deeply imprinted in your being. Let your ear lead you in classic Suzuki fashion, and put your mind to work remembering what you've heard. Later on, you can easily find a musically trained person (such as a choir director or an instrumentalist) to write down the notes for you as you sing them.

Of course, there are a variety of possible tones for any psalm. That's where your inner artist comes in. Listen carefully to how the word sense and line sense come together; whether the mood is major or minor; whether the psalm's inherent pattern is best served by a simple, repetitive tone or a more complex one that draws longer sections of text together. All of these characteristics are opportunities for your own sensitivity and creativity to come into play. As in all songwriting, you'll know when you've got it right. A happy melding of words and melody will virtually sing itself.

If you want to set a psalm to one of the tones in your notebook, how do you go about it? It's a simple three-step process:

1. Determine the number of lines in your psalm verse (two, three, four, five, or six), and choose a tone that will match. Note that sometimes verses that look like couplets can be combined into larger units.
2. Point the lines to discover where the reciting tone naturally wants to give way to the cadence formula. As we've seen, this can often be done in your head.
3. Sing your psalm tone and let your ear tell you if it works.

Adapting New Psalm Translations for Chanting

In chapter 6, I mentioned Nan Merrill's *Psalms for Praying: An Invitation to Wholeness.* Merrill's psalter became an instant hit with our weekly contemplative prayer group, and several of our members asked me if I could adapt her translation of Psalm 134 to a psalm tone suitable for chanting before Centering Prayer. In this case, it was simple to do, since the psalm is short and fairly regular in its line length.

You can follow the same steps I did to come up with a psalm tone that will match the sense of the poetry. First, read the psalm aloud several times to see if the individual lines seem to group into verses, and if so, of what length and regularity. This is crucial information to help you determine whether to look for a couplet (two-line) tone or to try one of the longer-line (expandable) psalm tones. In this case, with a little finagling, I could make the psalm fit fairly easily into a four-line verse format (look just ahead to see how I did it).

Second, decide on the tone you want to use and point accordingly. In this case, I decided to use my own C-major tone, pointed as shown here. You can listen to the results on track 28 of your CD. [CD track 28] ◉

> *Odd line* Come, bask in the Light \ of Love
> *Even line* All you who would serve / God's plan[2]
> *Odd line* Lift up your hands to the Ho\ly One
> *Last line* / Singing \ songs of praise
>
> *Odd line* Bow down and re\ceive blessing
> *Even line* from the Giver / of Life
> *Odd line* All praises be \ to You,
> *Last line* Whose Love created hea\ven and earth.

You'll find, however, that most of Merrill's new translations won't yield quite so easily. As I scanned her Psalm 13, for example, I could see that it would eventually point to the two-line Anglican tone. But to smooth it into somewhat regular two-line verses required a bit of recomposition of my own. Here's Nan Merrill's original:

> How long, my Beloved?
>   Will you forget me forever?
> How long will you hide your
>   face from me?
> How long must I bear this pain
>   in my soul,
>   and live with sorrow
>   all the day?
> How long will fear rule my life?
>
> Notice my heart and answer me,
>   O my Beloved,
> enlighten me, lest I walk as
>   one dead to life;

Lest my fears say,
    "We have won the day";
Lest they rejoice in their strength.

As I trust in your steadfast
       Love;
    my heart will rejoice,
        for in You is freedom.
I shall sing to the Beloved
    who has answered my prayers
        a thousand fold!
Come, O Beloved, make your home
        in my heart!

Here is my revision, set to its psalm tone. You'll find it on track 29 of
your CD. [CD track 29] ◉

How long, my Be / lov-ed?
Will you forget \ me forever?
How long will you hide your / face from me?
How long must I bear this pain \ in my soul?

How long must I live with / sorrow?
How long will fear \ rule my life?

Notice my heart and answer me, O my
    Be / lov-ed;
Enlighten me, lest I walk as one \ dead to life.
Lest my fears say, "We have won the / day";
Lest they rejoice \ in their strength.

As I trust in your steadfast / love,
My heart will re\joice in freedom.

I shall sing to the Be / lov-ed
Who has answered my prayers a \ thousandfold.
Come, O my Be / lov-ed,
Make your home \ in my heart.

As you can see, the art is simply one of selective recomposition—as little as is absolutely necessary—to make the new words flow into the pattern you've decided will suit them best. Once this step has been done, the rest is simply what we've practiced before, choosing the most graceful tone and pointing accordingly.

Creating Your Own Antiphons

In chapter 10, I introduced you to the wide world of antiphons. These short, eminently singable melodies, which encase their respective psalm texts like the bread in a "psalm sandwich," are used to highlight the theme of the psalm (rather like a musical callout) or to link the psalm to a particular season of the liturgical year.

Antiphons are a time-honored way to customize your psalmody. At its best, monastic psalmody has always been a dynamic interplay between the timeless rhythms of the psalms themselves and the individual spirit of a particular worshipping community. Antiphons carry the "spirit of particularity," and once you catch on to the basic principle, it's both easy and enormously satisfying to write your own.

During the three years I was director of the Contemplative Centre on Salt Spring Island, British Columbia, we had an active antiphon-writing group. The group came into existence spontaneously from the takeoff point of matching psalm tones to familiar hymns and carols. Just as I described in chapter 10, I'd introduced the subject of antiphons to the group using Psalm 100, "Shout with joy to the Lord, all you lands," decked out in its Easter antiphon, "Be not afraid; go tell my friends to set out for

Galilee." One member of our group listened carefully and suddenly had a bright idea: "Couldn't you do the same thing using 'Jesus Christ Is Risen Today' as the antiphon?"

He was right. You can hear how well the combination works by listening to track 30 on your CD; both thematically and musically, it's a match. [CD track 30] ⦾ From there the group was off and running. "What would be a comparable antiphon for the Christmas season," someone wondered; someone else immediately came up with, "Why not 'Joy to the World'?" We quickly went on to match Psalm 63 (see chapter 10) with "O Come, O Come, Emmanuel," and Nan Merrill's Psalm 134 (above) with the refrain from "Angels We Have Heard on High" (*Gloria in excelsis deo*). It was good fun and helped us connect our psalmody with the festival mood of the season.

When Christmas had come and gone, people were so enthusiastic about the process that they decided to continue the exploration. We wondered what interesting sources for new antiphon texts would be. Here are a few of the ideas we brainstormed together:

- Developing a set of antiphons based on the Beatitudes (Matthew 5:12ff). We saw this set as being particularly appropriate for use during Epiphany (the liturgical season between Christmas and Lent) when the emphasis is on letting one's light shine in the world.
- Developing a set of antiphons based on the short sayings of a favorite spiritual writer. Thomas Merton was our candidate of choice, but other lively contenders were Thomas Keating, Julian of Norwich, Hildegard of Bingen, and the Sufi mystic Rumi.
- Developing a set of antiphons based on an important spiritual theme, such as love, mercy, or forgiveness.
- Developing a set of antiphons featuring the voices and insights of women. Our group actually brought this project to completion

using Nan Merrill's translations to provide the antiphon for the same psalm translated traditionally. The effect was a fascinating counterpoint (and a welcome counterbalance) to the oftentimes aggressively male energy of the Psalms.

These suggestions are merely intended to prime the pump of your own imagination. But wherever your inspiration leads you, you'll want to keep the following parameters in mind. First, look for a text that's short and compelling. Antiphons have a way of working themselves deeply into your subconscious, from which they emerge, when needed, as small musical "wake-up calls." Remember my story of finishing up my day's ordeal down in the pump house, only to find myself singing the antiphon from vigils that morning: "With joy you will draw water from the fountain of salvation!" This kind of interplay happens most easily if the text is kept short—no more than a single line and perhaps even a single phrase.

Second, when it comes to developing the tune, remember that antiphons want to be singable. Keep your melody simple and tuneful. If you like, you can borrow from a popular song or a well-known hymn tune; it's been done many times before. For example, one of the most famous medieval antiphons, *Perspice christicolae*, is none other than the popular folk song "Summer Is Y-Cumen In." This is the medieval equivalent of setting an antiphon to a Beatles tune.

The other important musical concern to keep in mind is that the melody selected for the antiphon needs to match the mode of the psalm tone. Here again, I could get into a technical discussion of the medieval church modes, but your own ear will tell you most of what you really need to know. You already intuitively recognize major and minor mode from what's left of the old modal system in modern music. While the subject is a bit more complicated than that, major and minor will do well enough to get you started. Just remember that a psalm tone in the major mode (such as Psalm 100) wants to be matched with a major mode antiphon; a minor mode psalm tone (such as Psalm 63) wants a minor mode antiphon. As in the fashion world, mixing and matching is a time-tested principle, but only within a compatible color palette.

With the foregoing principles in mind, you have everything you need to begin customizing your psalmody, making it your own "joyful noise to the Lord." Over time, you can develop your own "house psalter" with translations that reflect your own spiritual taste and creativity. Not only is this process personally satisfying, it's also deeply authentic to the tradition of psalmody itself and, in fact, integral to its continued vitality. Sometimes we get the idea that sacred texts are cast in stone, like the Ten Commandments—too sacrosanct and perfect to alter a single word. But from the beginning, the psalms have been a creative interplay between timeless truth and the particularity of the human heart. Your own creative engagement is essential to bringing them alive; once they have come alive in you, they will almost inevitably further stimulate your own creative engagement. This is the inner magic of psalmody, known to all who have sincerely accepted the invitation the psalms extend. If you let the process unfold in you, you may be astonished where it leads you. But one thing is certain: you'll know the place when you get there.

 13

DEVELOPING YOUR OWN DAILY OFFICE

I F YOU'VE MADE IT THIS FAR, everything you need to make chanting the psalms a part of your regular daily practice is now in place. You're familiar with the basic principles of contemplative psalmody. You've learned how to pick up simple chant tones by ear, navigate the musical notation, and adapt and improvise your own psalm tones and antiphons. This chapter is about pulling it all together. We'll be looking at how to consolidate these separate skills into a regular practice of chanting the Divine Office.

The first order of business is a simple reassurance: You can do it! Even if you're on your own—with no monastery or spiritual journey group or anybody else who's interested nearby—you can still chant the psalms, and your spiritual practice will grow. True, in the traditional way of doing things, the Divine Office was a communal activity, and community undeniably adds an important dimension to the experience. But the lion's share of transformational work is carried out simply by having the willingness to

show up and start chanting. Breath, tone, and intentionality—three of the
four sacred elements we spoke of earlier—are there regardless of whether
you chant alone or with others. So are the purifying and heart-expanding
capacities we looked at in part one of this book, as the psalms become the
catalyst for the healing of your shadow material and the gradual awakening
of your unitive imagination. These powerful spiritual tools are available to
you right on your prayer stool as you simply open your Psalter and begin.

I've chanted the psalms every morning and evening for nearly thirty
years now. While some of this chanting has been shared with others during retreats or at monasteries, most of it has been right in my own living
room. It's so much a part of my daily routine that I can hardly envision life
without it. For what it's worth (which is actually a lot), I remind myself of
the hermit's secret: no prayer is ever offered alone. Even on a purely practical level, given the fact that Benedictine monasteries pretty much dot
the globe, it's a safe bet that at whatever time you sit down to do your Divine Office, your chanting will coincide with some other monastic community offering up the same ritual. From a more mystical perspective, as
Saint Benedict observed, your chanting is always "in the presence of the
angels." Even if you think there's no one there but yourself, your willingness simply to be present in this way carries your chanting into what the
Quaker mystic Thomas Kelly called "great orbit as prayer," where human
and divine yearning meet in a hidden dynamism of grace that many see as
the real inner ground sustaining the outward, visible world.

So breathe deeply and honor yourself. You are not uninmportant. And
you are not alone.

Getting Started

As you begin to develop your Daily Office, the ground rule is to keep it as
simple as possible, at least initially. Most attempts to incorporate this

spiritual practice into everyday life are wrecked by setting out with an overly ambitious program. For most people it is simply not realistic to think in terms of recreating the full monastic office in its sevenfold splendor. Even the standard regimen of four psalms apiece, morning and evening, which I follow as an oblate of New Camaldoli Monastery, can be a bit much, particularly if you're adding it to an established discipline of daily meditation or lectio divina. The deck gets overloaded and inevitably collapses.

Instead, you might start with just a psalm or two in the morning and a psalm or two before heading to bed. The last office of the day is called compline, and from time immemorial Psalm 4 and Psalm 91 have been associated with it. As we practiced earlier, you can chant them on a monotone or a simple step-up, step-down tone.

If space in your day permits, a brief pause around midday helps to refocus your energy and recharges that dynamic tension between psalmody and daily life. The classic noonday psalm is 121 ("I lift up my eyes to the hills"), but in fact, any of the short, pungent psalms in the sequence from 121 to 128 offers a marvelous counterpoint to the slings and arrows of a typical workday.[1] If noontime doesn't work for you, remember that the traditional monastic little hours of terce in the morning and none in late afternoon correspond roughly with morning and evening rush hour. Again, the sequence of psalms between 121 and 128 offers a rich treasury of wisdom that can easily be committed to memory and chanted on the drive to and from work.

What I'm saying is don't try to copy the monastic office from the outside. Find your way from the inside. If you're new to psalmody, get used to singing a few psalms every day in whatever way works best for you. As you start absorbing the psalms inside you, they will begin to change the way you look at life, and your own awakening depths will guide you in what to do next. The ground rule is to start simply (or simply start), then build on what you can comfortably sustain.

Early morning and early evening—lauds and vespers—have been the traditional times for serious monastic psalmody, but these two offices can
also be the most challenging to incorporate into a daily schedule: not
only because they must be coordinated with the rhythms of others in
your household, but because they classically have variable psalms (that is,
the menu changes each day), and you'll need to develop some sort of system for organizing what you'll be chanting. We'll tackle that problem
shortly, but first of all—and again, out of concern for sustainability—I
strongly recommend that you take on these offices one at a time rather
than trying to establish them simultaneously. Start with whichever time
period works better for you. Morning is easier for most people, before
everyone else in the household rises, but for myself, I curiously discovered
a "hole" at about 5 P.M. (after the close of the day's activities but before
dinner preparation) where my evening office would easily fit. Once you
get one office up and running, you can see if the other one will gracefully
fit itself in. If it doesn't, don't force the issue. Either office is a serious spiritual engagement and a significant step-up in your practice of psalmody.

In a classic monastic office, the order of service for lauds and vespers
is as follows:

> Invocation and doxology
>
>> *O God, come to my assistance;*
>> *O Lord, make haste to help me;*
>> *Glory to the Father and to the Son and to the*
>>> *Holy Spirit,*
>> *As it was in the beginning, is now, and ever shall be.*
>>> *Amen.*
>
> Psalmody (two to four psalms)
> Scriptural reading

Canticle (*Benedictus* at lauds, *Magnificat* at vespers)
Intercessory prayers
Lord's Prayer
Dismissal

You can duplicate this sequence if you wish, but if you're mostly on your own and chanting the psalms as part of a personal spiritual practice, I would strongly recommend an alternative strategy:

Invocation
Short scriptural reading
Psalmody (with or without canticle)
Meditation

I realize that this combination and sequencing is nontraditional. In traditional monastic practice, meditation (alias *contemplatio*) was not a part of the Divine Office. It belonged to lectio divina and was typically done in the privacy of the monk's cell. But when monasticism is transposed to the outer world, my experience has been that the core pieces of the transformational strategy come together in a somewhat different way. The powerful, innate attraction between chanted psalmody and silence pulls you down very quickly into strong, rich silence. The chief operative here, I suspect, is the "unloading of the unconscious" that Thomas Keating talks about. The psalmody catalyzes the participation of the unconscious, then the meditation itself does the purifying work. Placing the reading after the psalmody, as is traditional, interrupts the pull toward the silence.

If even that much formal structure is more than your practice can comfortably sustain, simplify still further: psalmody followed by meditation. Begin with an invocation if you wish (it can be a simple, nonverbal sign of the cross as you sit down in your chair); chant one or two psalms, then sit for twenty to thirty minutes of Centering Prayer or whatever form of meditation you practice. When you emerge from silence, you may choose to conclude your office with the Lord's Prayer or a short closing prayer.

Whatever you do, build *some* silence into your Daily Office: if not a full-fledged meditation, then at least eight or ten minutes of quiet, non-conceptual prayer before you get up and go about your day. In fact, if you don't do this, (heretical as this may sound) I would otherwise advise you not to chant the Divine Office at all. Silence is essential for the psalmody to do its integrative work. Without it, your practice will tend to remain on the surface, merely another thing you do. If this "doing" should become cloaked in piety or self-righteousness (a real risk when things stay on the surface), then your practice can quickly move from ineffective to actively counterproductive. Allow your psalmody access to those deeper places within you where the transformative work really goes on.

Choosing Which Psalms to Chant

Once you enter the arena of offices with variable psalms, you'll need to develop some sort of game plan for the choice and arrangement of your psalmody. We looked at a few basic strategies in chapter 6, but let's revisit the issue now that we've explored the musical aspects involved.

When I began chanting the psalms back in 1979, I was living alone on a remote island off the coast of Maine and had little choice but to use the material immediately available, which was my Episcopal Psalter. It divides the psalms into a daily regimen: two offices per day (morning and evening), generally with three psalms per office. I simply followed that schedule as best I could. You can do the same. Since the psalms in this version are all arranged in two-line verses, they lend themselves very easily to the simple, two-line psalm tones, such as our Anglican tone (discussed in chapter 12) or the step-up, step down tones we practiced earlier.[2]

If you're chanting from the Grail Psalms, your psalms will point easily to any of the tones we looked at in the preceding chapter. The simplest strategy is simply to plow through in numerical order, following the basic formula of the Episcopal Psalter: 150 psalms divided by thirty days per month divided by two offices per day, with some adjustment for very long or very short psalms (three days are allotted to work through Psalm 119).

If you have a close connection with a particular monastic community, it might seem like a natural solution to follow their order of psalmody. Ideally, if you could lay hands on a copy of the house psalter, you could join in chanting all or part of the Daily Office. I say *could*, however, because this seemingly elegant solution turns out to be unworkable in most cases. For various reasons, monastery choir books are not available for purchase, and "borrowing" them—if only for photocopying—is a practice that's strongly frowned upon. A compromise solution is to jot down the numbers and order of the psalms for each office while you're on retreat. Once you're back home, you can chant the designated "psalms du jour" to whatever tones you like.[3]

You can easily get your hands on various musical collections of lectionary psalms, including those by Joseph Gelineau, Richard Proulx, David Haas, George Black, and any number of other outstanding contemporary composers (for specifics, consult the Selected Musical Resources section at the end of this book). But keep in mind that lectionary psalms are intended primarily for choral performance during the Sunday morning liturgy, not for a personal Daily Office. So you'll have some beautiful psalm tones to work with, but you'll still be faced with the task of adapting them to your specific needs and purposes.[4]

If chanting the psalms becomes a regular part of your spiritual practice, you will probably eventually wind up creating your own Daily Office, with a choice and arrangement of psalmody that reflects your unique circumstances and spiritual design. At first, this may seem like an impossibly enormous task, but if you break it down into its component parts and take it gradually, it will become a deeply enriching, ongoing project. (Remember, this is the process that monasteries have used to develop their offices.) Basically, it's a four-step operation:

1. Decide on the number of offices you are actually going to chant. Will you address vespers and/or lauds only, or will you try to add in one or two of the little hours, such as noonday prayer or compline? Be realistic and err on the side of sustainability.

2. Determine how many and which psalms you will sing at each office and what your cycle will be. As a basic guideline, you can always consult the Rule of Saint Benedict (chapters 8 through 19), which spells out the traditional order of psalmody in explicit detail.[5] Obviously, you will need to adapt this massive schedule to fit your own circumstances; use it for reference only and not for copying.

3. Decide on the specific psalm tones you'll be using and point accordingly.

4. Develop your own creative variations, as we explored in the last chapter, using antiphons and new translations.

Remember that your personal creativity is an indispensable element in this process. You may be intimidated at first and try to research the "right" way to do it. But the right way is the way that gets you singing the psalms on a regular basis and carries you deeper into your own awakening heart. If a combination of psalms or a particular translation appeals to you, by all means use it, even if it seems unconventional.

Do you have to do all 150 psalms? What about those cursing psalms? Well, you're on your own recognizance here. In point of fact, I know very few monastic houses that actually sing all 150 psalms, even counting the night office. You will inevitably be doing some editorial pruning. But resolve to push your own envelope, deliberately including psalms that are challenging and stormy as well as the light-filled and reassuring ones—for that is how psalmody works its transformative magic.

Developing your own personal psalter is a labor of love that can take years, or a lifetime, to complete. But as you do so, you discover that it *is* your lifetime, a portrait of your authentic spiritual being that's more meaningful than any diary or scrapbook. As I've emphasized throughout this book, the more you make the psalms your own, the more they will make you *their* own, awakening new depths of creativity and originality within you as you increasingly learn to look at life through the eye of your heart.

Chanting the Psalms with Your Meditation Group

As meditation continues to gain popularity among Christian practitioners, contemplative prayer groups are sprouting up everywhere. People come together to meditate, usually on a weekly basis, often remaining after the meditation for a time of reading or reflection together or to share their personal spiritual journeys. To frame this weekly gathering within the context of psalmody can have a profound effect on the depth and vitality of the silence.

In most Centering Prayer groups, the practice of beginning the meditation with a designated lector reading a psalm is already in place. It is a simple step to move from this to having the entire group chant the psalm. The words will need to be distributed in advance, of course—people can pick up a copy as they enter the prayer room—and the chanting will need to be of the utmost simplicity. A monotone chant with organum will usually be easy enough for the entire group to grasp and powerful enough to create a profound entry point into the silence.

In part three of this book, we will also be looking at some new forms of Christian chanting that use the psalms in new ways, much more akin to classic mantric chanting. These work particularly effectively with meditation. But as I remarked earlier, there is already a deep and dynamic attraction between psalmody and meditation, even traditional psalmody, with all its words and images. The two carry each other deeper. Particularly in Centering Prayer groups, there is sometimes a tendency to view meditation primarily as a private experience, a therapeutic gateway into one's own personal unloading of the unconscious and healing.[6] Chanting the psalms as a group immediately catapults the experience to higher transpersonal ground. The sheer physical experience of drawing breath together and working with those four sacred elements of breath, tone, intentionality, and community entrains the energy of the group and creates a much deeper experience of the prayer itself.

A friend of mine, an experienced practitioner of Centering Prayer, joined me for mediation one day. As we sat down on our prayer mats, I said, "Let's begin by chanting a psalm or two." So we did; then we went into our time of silence.

When we emerged, she said, "That made a real difference. In all these years of meditating, finally I know what *adoration* is all about."

 *Part Three*

CREATIVE
ADAPTATIONS

14

IS THERE CHANTING
beyond the
PSALMS?

As we have seen repeatedly throughout this book, the words themselves are of primary importance in Christian sacred chanting. And since 150 psalms translates into more than five thousand lines of sacred poetry, there are a lot of words to deal with. Classic Christian psalmody is an art of high intelligibility requiring focused attention and a willingness to engage with the images and emotions that the psalms offer up as the working laboratory for personal transformation.

By its sheer prolixity, the tradition stands somewhat at variance with many of the great universal traditions of sacred chanting—at least as they are commonly taught and practiced in the contemporary West.[1] Psalmody is not *zikr* ("prayer of remembrance") in the classic Sufi sense, in which the repetitive chanting of one of the ninety-nine names of God lifts the prayer to a level of ecstasy. Nor is it toning or mantric chant, as in some forms of

Hindu and Buddhist practice, working intentionally with the vibration of sounds and pitches to produce desired effects in the inner body. While the psalms are certainly considered by the church fathers to be a primary tool for "putting the mind in the heart," they are usually associated with the preliminary, or "purgative," phase of the transformative process, where they lay the groundwork for purifying the passions and awakening the heart's capacity to feel deeply about spiritual realities. The psalms in and of themselves are not classically intended to land one immediately in the contemplative state.

The Orthodox theologian Simeon the New Theologian (whom we met earlier in chapter 5) reflects the traditional view when he assigns psalmody to the second rung of his ladder of transformation (there are four altogether), by which the monk gradually ascends to the "perfect" state of contemplation. As Simeon sees it,

> Those who undertake to climb by these rungs do not begin with the top and then go down, but start from the bottom and go upwards. The method by which he who wishes to may raise himself off the earth and rise up to heaven is as follows: first, he must wrestle with his mind and tame his passions; second, he must practice psalmody, that is, pray with the lips, for, when passions are subdued, prayer quite naturally brings sweetness and enjoyment even to the tongue and is accepted by God as pleasing to him; third, he must pray mentally; fourth, he must rise to contemplation. The first is appropriate to beginners; the second to those who have already achieved some measure of success, the third to those who are drawing nigh to the last rungs of perfection, and the last to the perfect.[2]

Both Simeon's imagery and the teaching itself are solidly attested to within the classic spiritual traditions of both the Christian East and the Christian West. The contemplative state is to be approached only gradually, after thorough moral purification and a systematic training of the intellect and imagination.

Similarly, while one sometimes hears the Desert Fathers advocating the use a single short phrase as a form of active prayer, such as John Cassian's famous use of the versicle from Psalm 70 "O God, come to my assistance, O Lord make haste to help me", it would be a misreading of the tradition to interpret these phrases as mantras in the classic Eastern understanding—that is, as devices to quiet the mind; to the contrary, they are capsules of pure, concentrated emotion. The reason this little phrase works so marvelously, Cassian claims, is "because it carries within it all the feelings of which human nature is capable."[3] Where feelings run deepest, so, too, does prayer.

To express this same idea in classic spiritual terminology, Christian sacred chanting has traditionally been a *cataphatic* practice. This means that it engages the faculties—reason, memory, feeling, imagination, and will—which are the foundation of our usual, or egoic, sense of selfhood.[4] It is not intended to transcend or still the mind, plunging the participant into a direct experience of formless or unboundaried selfhood, as is characteristic of *apophatic* practice and a good number of the world's sacred chanting traditions. While ecstatic moments can and do happen during the psalmody, they are not the goal of the process nor do they express its primary purpose within the traditional program of Christian contemplative transformation. The primary purpose, as we have seen, is to surface and temper the shadow material within the personal unconscious while at the same time strengthening the analogical imagination and the aptitude for metaphorical perception. Within the Christian metaphysical framework, these two "heart" capacities are seen as necessary preconditions for a unitive seeing that does not simply dissolve the particularity of the created order into a grand "Oneness," but can instead flow out from this underlying Oneness into the infinite play of particularity.

It is important, then, when exploring the various worldwide traditions of sacred chanting, not to fall into the trap of comparing apples and oranges. Judged from the perspective of classic contemplative chanting, Christian psalmody may look unduly cerebral and rigorous. And yes, the mental operations do tend to put a damper on ecstatic experience (at least until the words and music are well in hand) and to retard the transition into direct, nondual perception. Within its own self-understanding, however, psalmody is working with a different piece of the transformational program—not contemplation per se, but the moral and emotional underpinnings through which contemplation becomes a fully integrated part of the experience of human personhood. It's all part of that sometimes frustrating but always rich dialectic through which Christianity holds the tension between the unboundaried and the finite; between pure consciousness and the fragile human soul who weeps, prays, loves, and dies.

Functionally, however, the sheer weight of the tradition and the skill level required to access it have some important consequences, which, as a teacher of Christian contemplative practice, I come up against continually. Historically, we've seen how Christian sacred chanting and Benedictine monasticism grew up intertwined, not only for spiritual reasons but for practical ones as well. The seven-times-daily rule of liturgical psalmody stipulated by Saint Benedict pretty much requires a full-time monastic lifestyle, while the actual art of singing "in such a way that our voices are in harmony with our minds"[5] is musically rigorous enough to warrant regular choir rehearsals. Certainly this is the case with Gregorian chant, one of the most sophisticated and musically demanding art forms ever created, but it's true even of the simpler forms of modern vernacular chant we've been looking at in the course of this book. By now, most of you have probably had plenty of opportunities to experience the challenges involved in chanting the psalms firsthand: keeping the musical line moving, finding the right intonation, singing ascending and descending lines without losing pitch or tempo. "Breath, tone, intentionality, and community" are not merely a nice formula; they describe a complex, fourfold deployment of attention that requires practice and concentration. Until a certain skill level is attained, the results are not likely to be an aesthetic triumph.

Practically, this means that it is very difficult to initiate people directly into the chanting of the Divine Office during introductory retreat weekends (unless they take place at an actual Benedictine monastery with the choir already in residence). Other traditional monastic practices translate remarkably smoothly to life beyond the cloister; in the course of a weekend, it's easy to create an authentic experience of contemplative prayer, lectio divina, and even mindfulness practice during physical work. But when it comes to contemplative psalmody, anything more complicated than Suzuki-style monotone chant tends to produce such negative initial results that people are turned off by the whole experience. Chanting the psalms requires commitment and regular practice. At the Contemplative Centre in British Columbia, we discovered that the only really satisfying solution was to develop an ongoing chant group that practiced together for an hour each week. This core group was then able to "hold the space" during retreat weekends, allowing newcomers to experience both the wisdom and the beauty of traditional contemplative psalmody prayed in monastic choir.

Given the continuing groundswell of the Christian contemplative reawakening, there have been a variety of responses emerging to the ongoing challenge of adapting traditional monastic chanting to the conditions of contemporary "monks in the world." One solution is to continue in the direction of simplification inaugurated by Vatican II: opting more and more for simple, uncomplicated psalm tones or for an increasing use of refrains for the choral parts, with the psalm tones themselves left in the hands of trained soloists. But even in simplified settings, preventing the words of a psalm from turning into molasses requires trained attention.

And limiting the participation of untrained singers to the refrains effectively eliminates most of the transformational alchemy of psalmody, which occurs when the words and images are actually "ingested" through the act of singing.

The other, far more radical, option amounts to a fundamental revision of the spirituality of Christian sacred chanting. For two thousand years, the terms *chanting* and *psalmody* have been so deeply intertwined as to be virtually inseparable. True, there are certain chants that are not psalms: mass settings, litanies, canticles, and (strictly speaking) antiphons, but the tradition has been so formed around the backbone of the Divine Office (and that, in turn, around the daily recitation of the psalms), that it is difficult to envision a form of Christian chanting not linked to the psalms and to their distinctive methodology of spiritual transformation.

But is this in fact *causally* so? What would happen if Christian chanting were repositioned within the whole program of spiritual transformation as a primarily apophatic practice intended to transcend ego consciousness rather than purify it? In other words, what if it were brought into line with the classic niche occupied by sacred chanting in the majority of the world's other great sacred traditions? This would not necessarily mean eliminating the psalms, but it would certainly entail thinning out the verbiage considerably and using the core phrases in a very different way.

Such a radical departure would probably never pass muster if brought before a theological tribunal. But it is, in fact, happening. In many communities and in fascinating, ad hoc ways, this "inconceivable" is actually taking shape as an inevitable and necessary experiment. It's all part of the continuing change and adaptation as the classic practices of contemplative monasticism find their way into the new wineskins of our own times and circumstances. The next three chapters will report on some significant experiments at work.

 15

TAIZÉ
CHANT

W HEN THE TINY COMMUNAUTÉ DE TAIZÉ came into existence
in the early 1940s as an experiment in Protestant monasticm, little did the original handful of brothers suspect that their most enduring
legacy would be a body of chant that would quietly revolutionize the way
Christians sing and pray together. But that's typical of the surprises in a
community that for sixty years now has been living "provisionally," trying
to be of service to both a Christianity and a world deeply divided.

The word *Taizé* (pronounced "tay-zay") is now most widely recognizable as the name for the style of chanting pioneered by this community.
But it's first and foremost a place: a small farming village in the Burgun-
dian hills of eastern France. To this place, during the darkest days of World
War II, came a young Swiss divinity student by the name of Roger Schutz,
who was impelled by a vision of forming a community "on account of
Christ and the Gospel."[1] He bought a tumbledown farmhouse and immediately plunged into the dangerous work of offering sanctuary to Jews and
other refugees fleeing the Nazi occupation. Denounced in 1942, he himself was forced to flee to Switzerland but returned in 1944 to reopen the

community with a small band of compatriots. By 1949, six brothers had joined the fledgling Communauté de Taizé.

From the start, the idea of reconciliation was front and center in Brother Roger's vision of community. Reconciliation among the nations shattered by the war was an obvious priority. But just as important to this young Swiss Protestant (his father was a Calvinist pastor) was reconciliation within the household of Christianity, so that everyone who called themselves Christians might experience themselves as one body in faith and love.

As the winds of change began to sweep the Church in the early 1960s, Taizé's message of reconciliation was in tune with the times, and the little community suddenly found itself "discovered." In increasing numbers, pilgrims—particularly young ones—began arriving at Taizé, attracted to the simple gospel hospitality and unfailing message of hope. "So many people showed up one Easter," Brother Roger recalls, "that we had to tear down the wall of the church to fit them all inside." Before long, the small farm-yard monastery had overspilled its stone walls and become a veritable tent city encamped in the adjacent pastures. By 1974 the community could no longer evade the enormity of the spiritual hunger or its own pivotal role in offering a response and decided to host its first Council of Youth.

It was in the process of preparing for an army of young pilgrims from all over the globe that the brothers came face-to-face with the question of what to do about community worship. Like most monastic communities, the liturgy at Taizé was rooted in the Divine Office, with the daily chanting (in French) of the psalms and liturgical prayers. But clearly the traditional monastic office was not up to the task of accommodating an estimated forty thousand visitors, many of whom would never have been exposed to this form of prayer and would be unfamiliar with both the language and the musical complexity. Was there a way to develop a simpler form of community prayer that would allow everyone present to participate meaningfully?

Brother Robert Giscard came up with what proved to be a stroke of genius when he introduced into community worship one evening the canon "Jubilate Deo" ("Rejoice in the Lord," the opening line of Psalm 100) by the sixteenth-century German composer Michael Praetorius. It was an instant hit! In the simple, repetitive singing of this joyous round, young people from all around the world discovered that they could make spontaneous, beautiful music together without scores and service books. A deeper language of the heart simply sang itself for hours on end, rocking the foundations of the community's Church of the Reconciliation and—unbeknownst at the time—planting the seeds of a musical revolution.

Ostinato Chant

Seeking to build on that initial breakthrough, the brothers contacted the composer Jacques Berthier, who had been recommended to them by Joseph Gelineau, another of the community's longtime admirers.[2] Working collaboratively, Brother Robert and Berthier took on the challenge the community had set for them: to create a simple but elegant new chant form that was grounded in scripture, accessible in multiple languages, straightforward enough to be sung easily by a congregation, but sophisticated enough to be capable of musical elaboration and complexity if the circumstances presented themselves. The solution to this puzzle turned out to be a whole new art form: ostinato chant.

The term *ostinato* is not new. A traditional ostinato is a simple tune or harmonic progression repeated continuously throughout a composition. Typically, it's found in the bass line (usually played instrumentally by an organ or a cello); its major purpose is to serve as the harmonic foundation for a more complex musical expansion in the upper voices. Like a cinder block foundation, it is useful but not terribly appealing in itself.

But Berthier's use of the ostinato form essentially stood tradition on its head. In Taizé chant, the ostinato becomes the center of interest, the main place where both the action and its deeper meaning unfold. The entire congregation sings the simple, repetitive melody (usually in two- or four-voice harmony or in canon), while optional vocal and instrumental soloists add the musical variety and expansion.

The following well-known Taizé song, "Bless the Lord, my soul," is a good basic example of how ostinato chant works. The text is from Psalm 103:[3]

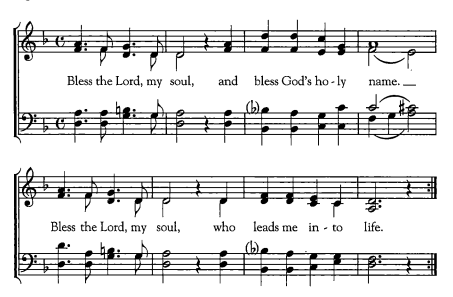

The congregation sings this simple acclamation over and over (typically, a single Taizé chant lasts for at least five and as long as ten minutes). Singers can opt to stay with a single musical line or try out all the parts. As the successive repetitions begin to weave a contemplative space, the song deepens into *zikr*-like prayer. The simple harmony can be held by keyboard or guitar accompaniment, but if instrumentalists are available, there are solo and duet parts for trumpet, trombone, horn, flute, clarinet, oboe, bassoon, cello, and recorder.[4]

The words for these short acclamations are basically scriptural, but the actual citations tend to be simplified and rephrased slightly so as to create a body of scriptural "pith sayings" that imprint themselves, together with the music, deeply in the unconscious. In addition to lines from the psalms, there are also numerous quotations from the teachings of Jesus and many original poems and prayers by Brother Roger and other members of the community.

Technically speaking, most of these new songs are antiphons (Berthier himself refers to them as "refrains"). But what makes these antiphons unusual is that they are not intended as complements to the psalmody (remember the psalm sandwich?) but as stand-alone compositions that essentially replace the psalmody.[5]

A Dead Language?

As I just implied, Taizé's real solution to the question of the language barrier lies in the repositioning of chanting as a form of contemplative prayer. When the words are made simple and fall deeply into a listening heart, the particular language in which they are chanted becomes far less of an obstacle. But in their original quest to find a common linguistic denominator for the new chants, Brother Robert and Jacques Berthier arrived (somewhat to their surprise) at Latin as the language of choice—deeply traditional and equally unfamiliar to all. In a wonderful irony, the "dead language" thrown out at Vatican II slipped back in at Taizé through practical necessity, where it has continued to demonstrate its utility as a vehicle for sacred chanting within the Christian tradition. Some of the most well-known songs in the Taizé repertory are in Latin, including *Veni, Sancte Spiritus* ("Come, Holy Spirit"), *O Christe, Domine Jesu* ("O Lord, Jesus Christ"), *Laudate, Omnes Gentes* ("Praise the Lord, all you Nations"), and the universally beloved *Ubi Caritas* ("Where love and charity abide, there God dwells").[6]

The fruitful partnership between Jacques Berthier and the Taizé community lasted for twenty years and produced one hundred chants before coming to an end with the composer's death in 1994 (Brother Robert Giscard had died in 1993). But new songs continue to be written as the community as a whole has taken on the work of expanding the repertory according to the well-tested template.

Options and More Options

Aleatory is another of those standard musical terms that was given a whole new spin at Taizé. Typically, it refers to music in which an element of chance is deliberately built into the structure of the composition—passages left for improvisation, alternative sequencing, or different instrumental and/or vocal combinations—so that each performance is a new and partially random combination of variables.

At Taizé, the word *aleatory* translates best as "open-ended." Most of the chants in the repertory exist in both simple and complex versions: as a basic ostinato chant and with a full complement of instrumental and vocal parts to support any combination of soloists who happen to show up. There is no such thing as a definitive score for any given chant. How it is performed at any given service will be a function of the personnel available.

All Taizé chants are to some degree aleatory, but perhaps the most striking in its range of complexity is the justly famous *Veni Sancte Spiritus*. The ostinato chant itself—a traditional Latin invocatory prayer—is succinct and mantralike:

In fact, this utterly simple chant can be simplified even further. It can be launched as a monotone chant, with all singers chanting the bass line in unison, either a cappella or accompanied by nothing more than a Celtic drum beating a steady heartbeat. (The word *Spiritus* means not only "spirit" but "breath," so this is a chant literally of and on the breath.) The three other choral lines can then be layered on; each one brings a subtle variation in the mood and tonal color. You can listen to the effect on track 31 of your CD. [CD track 3 1] ⊙

If musical forces are available, however, this same chant can swell to almost Mahleresque proportions. There are options for flute, oboe, clarinet, recorder duo, woodwind trio, trumpet, and even brass quartet, as well as vocal solos in five different languages. Like toppings on an ice cream sundae, any combination of the various instrumental and vocal options can be overlaid on the basic heartbeat of the ostinato—but not so heavily as to obscure the chanting itself or to dissolve into vocal cacaphony.[7]

Even the simplest songs in the Taizé repertory sometimes contain hidden possibilities for musical complexity. Take, for example, this simple four-measure canon, which we'll call theme 1:

But with all four voices entering one measure apart (notated in the score as A1, A2, B1 and B2), suddenly one finds oneself in the midst of a fairly complex polyphony. To make matters even more interesting, the song comes with its own countermelody, again in the form of a four-part canon, which we'll call theme 2:

The Lord is my light, my light and sal - va - tion: in God I trust, in God I trust. The

In its fullest musical complexity, this compact refrain turns into an eight-voice double canon, challenging and mentally exhilarating. But the song can also be sung in much simpler versions: as a two-part canon (one voice beginning theme 1 as the second moves to theme 2) or even as a chorale (with the two themes performed simultaneously). You can listen to some of these musical combinations on track 32 of your CD. [CD track 32] ◉ With Taizé chant, *better* doesn't necessarily mean "more complex." When the music is performed with sincerity and attention, it is entirely satisfactory at any skill level or degree of complexity.

The Spirituality of Taizé

Taizé chant is more than a musical form. The heart and soul of it lie the illumined vision of Brother Roger. *Light* is the word that comes most immediately to mind when describing the spirituality of Taizé. While I haven't done a formal word count, my hunch is that this word would show up with overwhelming frequency in the chants. Brother Roger's theology (and much of the poetry of the chants is his own) is of light shining in the darkness, of Christ as a ray of hope shining in the depths of every person and conferring the courage to face the darkness—both one's personal darkenss and the darkness of the world. The words of his most famous hymn make this message simple and eloquent:

> *Jésus le Christ, lumière intériere,*
> *Ne laisse pas mes ténèbres me parler;*
> *Jésus le Christ, lumière intérieure,*
> *Donne moi d'accueillir ton amour.*

> (Lord Jesus Christ, your light shines within me,
> Let not my doubts nor my darkness speak to me;
> Lord Jesus Christ, your light shines within me,
> Let my heart always welcome your love.)

This complete openness to the light shining even in darkness would ultimately carry him to a martyr's death. In August 2005, he was slain during evening prayer by a disturbed woman pilgrim who attacked him with a knife as twenty-five hundred horrified young pilgrims looked on. He was ninety years old. While tragedies such as this defy rational explanation, more than a few have commented on the Christ-like nature of his life and death and the striking resonance between his final self-oblation and the Paschal Mystery itself. Whatever the deep structure of reality may be, one senses that Brother Roger will continue to be a spiritual force as the path of reconciliation he embodied so fully continues to take root as the foundational morality of twenty-first-century consciousness. In a small but not insignificant gesture, the funeral mass was celebrated at Taizé by a Roman Catholic cardinal, with the liturgy of the Word read by an Anglican bishop and Protestant pastors, and the final prayers sung by an Orthodox bishop and archpriest. Communion was served to everyone regardless of denomination. It was a fitting tribute—and perhaps, one hopes, a foretaste of better things to come.

Around the world, Taizé chant has become almost a universal Christian language. I have chanted it on three continents, including a memorable impromptu service in the Upper Room in Jerusalem, where several converging tour groups spontaneously burst into a rendition of *Ubi Caritas*. Particularly in North America, churches of all denominations are undertaking "services in the style of Taizé," which seem to be replacing traditional evensong as the liturgy of choice for Sunday evening worship. If your church or contemplative prayer group is pondering taking on such a project, the following summary of the major points in this chapter can serve as a practical set of guidelines.

First, the music is easily available from GIA Publications in Chicago. The Taizé songbook is an inexpensive, paperbound booklet containing most of the ostinato chants.[8] The instrumental and solo accompaniments come in separate part books, which are also readily available.

The songbooks include basic instructions for the organization and logistics of such services. Typically, there are chants, scripture readings, five to ten minutes of silence, more chants, and intercessory and closing prayers. In many cases, the veneration of the cross is a prominent feature of the service, as it is at Taizé. A large cross is laid horizontally in the sanctuary, slightly elevated at its upper end. As the communal chanting holds the space, individuals are free to come forward and kneel beside the cross for a time of private prayer. Often provision is made for the lighting of a candle during this time. Votive candles and (increasingly) icons are ubiquitous props, in keeping with the overall Taizé theme of light.

Second, remember that Taizé chant is intended to be aleatory, or provisional. There is no single correct way of performing it. People typically think they need to round up instruments to create a full Taizé band, but this is not the case; the chants can be done simply with whatever instrumentation is on hand: a keyboard, a guitar, recorders, a clarinet. The combinations are all part of the charm (one of my all-time favorites was an ensemble consisting of a piano, bassoon, flute, and French horn). All of the instrumental parts do not need to be filled, and the vocal solos are always optional. In certain cases (which I'll get to shortly), Taizé can be performed beautifully with no accompaniment whatsoever. The backbone of the worship is ostinato chanting, and even in very simple format, it will draw a group deeply into the experience of contemplative prayer.

Third, it is important to keep in mind that while Taizé music offers a variety of performance options, it is *not* improvisational chant. (We will be looking at examples of this kind of chanting in the next chapter.) The harmonies themselves are written to very tight tolerances and should not be tampered with. I will speak more about this at the end of the chapter, but my suspicion is that Taizé is a highly conscious art, producing its desired effect not just through its theology, but through its tone palette and vibrations, as in classic Eastern chant. The harmonies are clean and light-filled, reminiscent of Bach and the French Renaissance. For the full effect, it's important to stay within the written score. Memorize it, to be sure, but don't expand on it.

Finally, allow time for the chants to be. As I mentioned earlier, authentic Taizé chanting goes on for at least five, sometimes ten, minutes per chant. This spaciousness allows time for people to sink deeply into the contemplative experience. I once knew a Protestant chaplain who insisted that each Taizé chant was to be done three times through—period. Such an attitude defeats the whole purpose of the art form.

Taizé Chant and Contemplative Prayer

While the primary use of Taizé chant is in the setting of community worship, some of the chants lend themselves particularly well to supporting small-group contemplative prayer. In this context, they function as what the Centering Prayer folks call a "vestibule," to usher the movement into and out of silence. In this format, the chanting is strictly a cappella—except, perhaps, for the "accompaniment" of a single note on the bell bowl to signal the beginning and end of the meditation period.

One chant that works particularly well in this format is *O Christe Domine Jesu* ("O Lord, Jesus Christ"). This tiny, four-measure acclamation turns out to be a classic Jesus Prayer, traditionally revered as the most powerful prayer a Christian can pray. It offers a profound way of centering the group and inviting this sacred presence into the meditation. When our contemplative group prays the chant in this fashion, we begin with the bass line alone sung in unison by all parts:

Once the group has settled into this unison chanting, the other lines can be added (soprano, then alto, then tenor) to create the full, beautifully simple harmony. Go to track 33 on your CD to hear how this is done. [CD track 33] ⊙

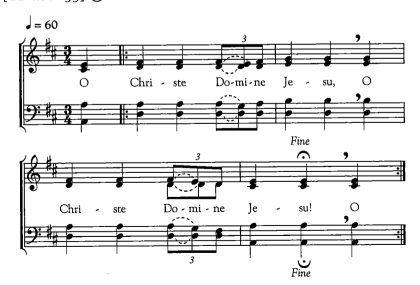

This chant seems to have a particular affinity with Centering Prayer;

I am always struck by how the "color" of the harmony (as gently golden warmth, as my inner eye seems to see it) matches the basic tonal color of Centering Prayer. The chant *Confitemini Domino* ("We trust in the Lord") is another close tonal match to Centering Prayer. *Veni Sancte Spiritus* also lends itself extremely well to this type of vestibule usage—obviously in the simpler form described earlier in this chapter—although its tonal color seems to match up much better with the slightly more austere inner modality of Christian Meditation than with Centering Prayer.[9] For use in this setting, the chants must be ultrasimple so as not to cause excessive mental activity as the group moves in and out of deep meditation.

A Quiet Revolution

I must admit that I've met relatively few church choir directors who find Taizé chant interesting. From the standpoint of most contemporary musicians, Taizé is boring. It simply repeats itself (over and over and over . . .), offering little in the way of harmonic elaboration and variation, those two cornerstones on which so much of Western sacred music is built.

But from the point of view of the renewal of Christian life, Taizé is anything but boring. The genius of this music is that it makes the experience of deep common prayer easily accessible. The chanting is so simple and yet so profound that few can resist its spell as they enter in and allow themselves to be carried down into their own depths. The mental noise quiets down. Worship truly becomes worship.

At Saint Benedict's Monastery in Colorado, the monks have been using Taizé chant for well over a decade to create an effective buffer zone for Sunday morning Mass. Needing a way to quickly integrate overstimulated visitors from the wider community into the silence and contemplative pace of Trappist worship, they hit on the solution of beginning worship with five minutes of Taizé chanting. It works like magic! As the chant takes hold, the group quickly settles down and enters the stillness. From there, the monks move into the traditional Sunday morning psalmody and Mass, but with a congregation that is collected enough to participate fully.

The quieting effect is only the tip of the iceberg, however. For as the mental noise settles down, so, too, do the judgments and criticisms and is-sues—the theological and institutional polarization that keeps Christians alienated from one another and from the family of world religions. Per-haps this has been the most surprising discovery of the sixty-year-old ex-periment at Taizé: the fact that the contemplative level is where reconciliation really begins to happen, as people discover their real one-ness at a greater depth of heart.

I, too, love the complexity of a good Bach cantata, but I recognize that the "little springtime" of Taizé (as Pope John XXIII dubbed it) is just that, and there is far more going on in this chant than meets the eye. For some reason—whether it lies in the chanting itself or in some mysterious heal-ing power in the particular vibrational spectrum of the Taizé harmonic palette—this music points the way to higher ground. In every place I've seen it tried, it has rapidly created a more heartfelt, grounded, and inclu-sive Christianity. I suspect that, as with Gregorian chant, we may be wit-nessing yet another case of objective art whose origins are really "from above."

Be that as it may, for more than half a century, Taizé has been on the leading edge in the field of Christian contemplative chanting, creating not simply a new body of music, but a whole new approach to how chant-ing works to support the transformation of the heart. Far closer to the sa-cred traditions worldwide, it appears to be a supremely serviceable vehicle as the school for the Lord's service envisioned by Saint Benedict moves beyond the walls of the monastery. It has clearly earned its place as a core building block of a new and universal contemplative Christian consciousness.

SONGS
of the
PRESENCE

W E ARE SITTING IN A CIRCLE on our prayer stools and cushions, about a dozen of us, in the beautiful small oratory at the Episcopal House of Prayer in Minnesota. We are about to begin a time of sacred chanting and silent meditation. After the three long chimes on the bell bowl, our worship leader begins a slow, repetitive chant:

The group picks up the chant, and for a minute or so, all in the room are singing in unison. Then one member adds a variation. Listen to it on track 34 of your CD. [CD track 34] ⊙

She has introduced harmony at the minor second, together with a slight melodic variation. This close, intentionally discordant harmony adds a distinctly Middle Eastern flavor, and for another minute or so, the group continues to chant in this new tonal color. Then, as the momentum around this impulse begins to fade, another person introduces a major third, completely shifting the feeling of the song, and still another person quickly picks up the new tonal color and adds the fifth. You can follow these harmonic variations on track 34.

As the group relaxes into this full major mode harmony, the volume spontaneously increases. People try out the different voice parts, and the simple musical lines shift and shimmer like a kaleidoscope. Then, just as spontaneously, the fifth drops out, and the chant grows softer. Someone in the group shifts the third back to the minor second, and the chant becomes softer yet. Finally, everyone returns to the single, monotone chant, which continues on the breath for another few recitations, and then, as if by an unspoken synergy, comes to a halt. The bell bowl rings again, and everyone enters silence.

There are no musical scores to be seen anywhere, but, no, the group is not singing from memory. This is a spontaneous happening, an improvisation that comes into being as the participants, in tune with both the chant and each other, mutually explore its harmonic possibilities. Rather like a flock of birds all swooping together in flight, this is an experiment in spontaneous presence to a guiding intelligence deeper than the mind.

"Songs of the Presence" is, in fact, the name by which this new repertory of chants has come to be known. They represent a promising new experiment in another nontraditional form of chanting being developed collaboratively by a group of contemporary Christian Wisdom teachers to support an emerging Christian consciousness that is both more contemplative and more interspiritually attuned.[1]

The catalyst and unofficial leader of this exploration is the Reverend Lynn Bauman, director of the Praxis Retreat and Learning Center in Elwood, Texas. (We met him earlier in this book, as the author of *Ancient Songs Sung Anew*, a new dynamic translation of the psalms.) Bauman and his family lived in Iran for more than a decade during the 1960s and 1970s while he taught and studied at the University of Teheran. There he was deeply influenced by Near Eastern styles of sacred chanting, particularly Islamic *zikr*, or "prayer of remembrance," through which he saw people being drawn simply and effortlessly into a profound experience of the divine. When he returned to North America, Bauman began to adapt this form of chanted prayer to a Christian milieu. The calming and deepening effect was so instantaneous that people immediately began clamoring for more.

One of his first experiments along these lines is still among his most popular. Building on an inspiration from the popular Franciscan teacher Richard Rohr,[2] he took the key line from Psalm 46 ("Be still and know that I am God") as the basis for a simple monotone chant, but with one small variation: each time the line is repeated, key words are taken away. The result is a "funnel-like" effect that leads straight down into silence:

> Be still and know that I am God
> Be still and know that I am
> Be still and know
> Be still
> Be

This chant can be sung in unison. But harmony will often arise spontaneously as people add organum (singing the same tune a fourth below or fifth above, as we learned to do in chapter 8) and sometimes the major third, creating a classic tonic chord. Each phrase expresses its own unique meaning and understanding as the prayer moves toward utter simplicty. It is a profound and highly effective way to lead a group into silent prayer, as well as a good introduction to this new form of improvisational chanting.

The experiment gathered momentum in the summer of 2001, when Bauman teamed up with Philip Roderick, a Welsh Wisdom teacher, and

David Keller, director of the Episcopal House of Prayer in Minnesota, to produce more than two dozen new improvisational chants. Keller's spiritual director, Father Thomas Hand, S.J., also contributed several chants. The chants were recorded in performance by the choir of All Saints Episcopal Church in Corpus Christi, Texas, and released on a CD titled *Songs of the Presence*.[3] Since that time, the work has been taken up by others, and the repertory has grown considerably. New chants have been contributed by David Stringer, Ward Bauman, and a few by myself, and a second CD is in preparation.

Improvisational Chant

Like Taizé chant, this new body of chants works on the principle of repetition. A short phrase or sentence is sung continuously, creating the ostinato chant effect of drawing the prayer deeper. Unlike Taizé, however, the Songs of the Presence are intentionally improvisational. The chant tune is a simple melody set within an implicit harmonic pattern. The full realization of the chant's potential depends on each group hearing the harmonic possibilities and unfolding them spontaneously in the synergy of the moment. Every chant is its own unique and unrepeatable event.

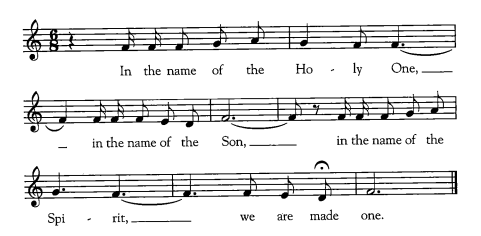

A simple, major mode melody lies in the background of the invoca-tory prayer by David Keller on the facing page.

Most people will very quickly pick up the implicit "six-four" harmony (harmony based on the major sixth chord) by ear. Again, you can listen to this on track 35 of your CD. [CD track 35] ◉

A much more complex range of possibilities lies within the following beautiful tune by Thomas Hand. The rose is the biblical symbol of inner opening and enlightenment, used to represent both Jesus and the Virgin Mary, but even more intimately, the mysterious unfolding of one's own soul:

Slow-ly blooms the rose with-in, slow-ly blooms_the rose with-in.

On track 36 of your CD, you'll hear the improvisations that arose spontaneously as our singers worked with this chant. [CD track 36] ◉

These melodic and harmonic variations are quite lovely, and you are welcome to try them for yourself. But please remember that this is not a "find the right answer" kind of situation where there is an implicitly "cor-rect" performance that participants must memorize beforehand or deduce on the spot. The essence of this style of chanting is that the harmonies will emerge spontaneously from the particular chemistry of each group. A group with trained musicians may hear and be able to reproduce a more complex range of harmonic options. But simplicity—even to the point of remaining on the unison chant line[4]—also serves the purpose, which lies in yielding the heart to the power of the chant-prayer to draw the heart deeper.

Creating Your Own Chants

While the repertory of Songs of the Presence is growing, the most impor-tant aspect of this experiment not the product but the process itself. As the old saying goes, "If you give a person a fish, he'll eat for a meal; if you teach him to fish, he'll eat for a lifetime." The real possibilities of this new art form are realized as individuals and groups learn to create their own chants out of short texts and teachings that engage their attention. The experiment is really about giving permission to a basic creative spark that is already inherent within the words themselves.

At a retreat in British Columbia, for example, we were working with the Gospel narrative of Jesus walking on the water (John 6:16–24.) To calm the terror of his disciples, Jesus offers the powerful reassurance, "Take heart; it is I; do not be afraid."

We realized that sounded like a potent mantra—particularly so if the "it is I" gets shortened to "I am" (the two phrases are interchangeable in the original Greek). We came up with the spoken chant: "Take heart; I am; do not be afraid." Very quickly, the following melody formed itself; you can hear it on track 37 of your CD. [CD track 37] ◉

Take heart; I am; do not be a - fraid. Take

The group was off and running, with some lovely harmonies emerging spontaneously. We used this small chant as a theme song for the whole retreat and as a way of entering into both meditation and lectio divina.

As we've just seen, the three-step process for creating a chant is utterly simple:

1. Find or create a scriptural "pith saying" that seems suitable for chanting.
2. Come up with a simple, rhythmic melody (it can consist of only two or three notes, or even a monotone).
3. Chant it together as a group and see what harmonic and melodic variations spontaneously emerge out of the prayer.

Potential candidates for this sort of treatment are limited only by your imagination. Lines from the psalms, Gospel images ("I am the vine, you are the branches"; "You are the salt of the earth"; "Come, follow me"), phrases from the liturgy, and even single core words (*awake, rejoice*) all come immediately to mind. And beyond the Bible lies a whole world: quotes from poets and mystics of the Christian tradition and of other great sacred traditions, such as Rumi, the Bhagavad Gita, and the Tao Te Ching.

Toward a Greater Inclusivity

Because these chants gravitate toward what is deepest and most universal in the human spirit, they have become primary vehicles to support the emerging interspiritual consciousness of our times. Remember in chapter 3, when I mentioned the interfaith worship service in Vancouver, in which the chant "Holy, Holy, Holy One" caught on and swept through the crowd, holding worshippers spellbound for more than an hour? That chant is one of the original Songs of the Presence, contributed by Father Thomas Hand. "There is nothing but God, there is only God," the chant with which this chapter began, is actually a translation of the Islamic "*La illaha illala*," and one of the most beautiful chants in the repertory comes from a line in the Koran, "Wherever you turn, there is the face of God."

Chants such as these witness profoundly to the fact that there is nothing to fear from participating deeply in the sacred mantras of another religious tradition; beneath the superficial barriers of language and theology, it is all one heart. The chants provide a fruitful ground where people can begin to experience this universal heart firsthand and nurture the inner awakening that leads to outer reconciliation.

Performance Options

These chants are created ideally for small group worship in which there is alternation between simple chanted prayer and meditation. At Wisdom schools, they have become the official form of morning and evening prayer, supporting the natural movement of the spirit from adoration into silence. For harmonic improvisation to reach its full potential, the group needs to be seated in a circle; since the chant is intended to flow directly into silent prayer, people should already be seated on their prayer stools or mats or on chairs.

A typical order of service would include the following:

> Opening chant(s)
> Reading of scripture, lectio divina style[5]
> Chanting
> Silent meditation
> Chanting
> Closing prayer

The chants also work well in a simpler format, as an entry into and exit from meditation. In this case, the format is simply chant/silent meditation/chant. In either case, the essential transformative magic of ostinato chanting remains the same. As the group begins to center its energy in the heart, an attunement emerges that expresses itself both outwardly in the beauty of the music and inwardly in the suppleness of the spirit. In this state, both prayer and meditation flow far more easily.

Reclaiming Fullness

The Songs of the Presence experiment grew out of a desire to create a more mystical and fully embodied experience of sacred chanting within a Christian milieu. As with Taizé chant, the sense was that simplification was the order of the day; the verbal and intellectual barriers that block access to the immediate transformative power of sacred chanting needed to be stripped away. This new repertory of chants is in some ways even more radical than Taizé in that there are no musical scores at all. My own efforts to transcribe some of the music for this book comprise the first time this music has emerged out of oral tradition (perhaps a dubious distinction). The intent is to create a body of songs that teach themselves virtually instantaneously and point the way toward those silent depths that lie beneath the surface structure of the mind. An ancient Byzantine prayer expresses the idea beautifully and offers perhaps the best rationale for this kind of work. You can chant it yourself, using our familiar Anglican tone.

> Serene light shining in the ground of my being,
> Draw me to yourself;
>
> Draw me past the snares of the senses,
> Out of the mazes of the mind;
>
> Free me from symbols, from words,
> That I may discover the signified,
>
> The word unspoken in the darkness
> That veils the ground of my being.

 17

IONA CHANT
and GOUZES
CHANT

I T IS IMPOSSIBLE IN A BOOK of such relatively brief scope to keep up with all the new developments in Christian sacred chanting during an era of unprecedented change and innovation. But it would be remiss not to at least mention two other contemporary movements, both of them European in origin, that are having considerable impact on the shape of the future: Iona chant and Gouzes chant.

Iona Chant

By its own self-understanding, Iona chant is not chant. It is songs, and its Protestant composers take pains to distinguish this new musical genre from either the classic Roman Catholic liturgical chanting or contemporary contemplative chant forms such as Taizé.[1] But its contemplative spirit is immediately apparent to all who participate in it, and by whatever name, the music of Iona has become a major player in the renewal of contemporary Christian chanting.

Iona chant comes from the Iona Community, a contemporary Protestant revival of the ancient monastic tradition on this venerable "holy isle" off the west coast of Scotland. The spiritual roots go deep on Iona. The first monastery was established there by the Irish monk Saint Columba in the year 563, some thirty years before Christianity arrived in Britain. For nearly six centuries, Iona was a stronghold of Celtic Christianity, maintaining its identity long after the Irish Church had formally disappeared.[2] Toward the end of the twelfth century, the site was converted to a Benedictine abbey, which endured for another four centuries before finally falling victim to the Protestant Reformation. After a hiatus of nearly four hundred years, spiritual community was again revived on Iona in 1938, when the restored abbey become home to a small residential community offering hospitality to pilgrims and services twice a day in the abbey church.

The mission of this new Iona Community, however, is not to revive monasticism or recreate the experience of yesteryear. The goal is to renew the Christian life itself by restoking the fires of mystical and prophetic vision. The community is intentionally open-ended: visitors come and go, carrying home with them an expanded spiritual horizon and a powerful new repertory of songs to support them in the journey.

The principal creative force behind Iona chant is John Bell, who heads up the Wild Goose Worship Group, the community's composition and publication task force. Perhaps surprisingly, the songs are not actually composed on Iona. Bell resides in Glasgow (in keeping with the community's expanded vision of membership), and he takes irreverent delight in announcing that most of these hauntingly atmospheric melodies originated "in an overcrowded living room next to one of the most heavily polluted arterial roads in the city."[3] But while he vigorously debunks any attempt to drape a monastic ambience around his songs ("There have been no monks on Iona for over four hundred years," he reminds his audiences), the Celtic spirit pours through the music from his heart and soul.

As the musical mainstays of daily worship at the abbey, these songs are a Celtic monastery in their own right.

There are many initial similarities between the Iona Community and Taizé. Both began as Protestant movements toward reclaiming a simpler, more Gospel-oriented Christianity. Both have developed a similar worship style, featuring a simplification of the liturgy and short, singable chants to encourage movement out of the head and into the heart.

But there are significant differences as well. Whereas Taizé is deliberately meditative chanting intended to lead into contemplative prayer, Iona is decidedly "not just for people who are into meditation," according to Bell.[4] In fact, while acknowledging the important contributions of Taizé chant, he does not cite it as an influence on his work. His sources lie primarily within his Scottish tradition of simple, harmonized songs and in the nursery rhymes and songs from childhood with their uncomplicated, rhythmic repetitions. He also draws extensively from the songs of the indigenous churches of South Africa and from other sacred traditions as farflung as the Latin American charismatic assemblies and the Russian Orthodox Church. He warns people against singing these songs over and over "à la Taizé" (twice through is the standard prescription). The Iona tradition is definitely cataphatic, and its intended fruits are more in prophetic engagement than in contemplative stillness.

The selection of songs in the various Wild Goose hymnals corresponds to traditional Christian liturgical categories. There are songs for gathering, to accompany confession, to announce the proclamation of the Gospel, for use during intercessory prayer and Communion, and for closing. There are also the standard mass chants (Kyrie, Gloria, Agnus Dei, Alleluia, Dona Nobis Pacem, and the like).

Typically, an Iona song will be a short (eight- to sixteen-measure) hymn in four-part harmony, such as the following "leaving" song (that is, for closing worship).[5] You'll find it on track 38 of your CD. [CD track 38] ⊚

Take, O take me as I am; sum - mon out what I shall be; set your seal up-on my heart and live in me.

Iona chant tends to be much more rhythmic than Taizé, in keeping with its African and Latino influences. Dotted and syncopated rhythms abound, and frequent use is made of a call-and-response format, both between cantor and congregation and within the musical voice parts themselves. But as Bell attests from long experience, these lively rhythms come naturally to the ear (they only cause trouble when sight-reading gets involved), and the melodies are expressly designed to be easy to teach and sing. He reports how, at a 1993 Easter broadcast live from Iona Abbey, a congregation that had never heard one particular song before learned it thirty minutes before the broadcast—in four-part harmony and completely by ear. Even the most musically sophisticated of the Iona songs fall easily within the reach of the average amateur singer.

While the songs are not primarily contemplative in their intent, they have earned a place in the hearts of contemporary contemplatives because of their profound musical and mystical beauty. Look closely, for example, at "Take, O take me as I am." The text rests on an image from the Song of Songs ("Set me as a seal upon your heart"); in the context of a closing song, it expresses a powerful recommitment to the journey of ongoing transformation. The final chord is a stroke of pure genius. It doesn't resolve but ends with the final note in the alto line (C, or "ti" in the major scale) pressing against the D-flat (or "do," the key in which the piece is written) in a haunting dissonance that seems to suggest the journey itself: untidy but open-ended. The sheer magic of moments such as these makes these songs shine like gems in the repertory of contemporary Christian sacred chanting.

Gouzes Chant: Ancient Songs Sung Anew

For the past two and a half chapters we have been exploring life beyond psalmody. My contention has been that the contemporary movement toward greater simplification and spiritual inclusivity has left the psalms a bit in the lurch, at least as the backbone of Christian sacred chanting. We've seen how psalmody has classically been tied to a monastic form of Christianity, not easily adaptable to the conditions of daily life beyond the cloister walls.

Yet what remains unmentioned in all this is the power of psalmody to create *new* monastic community: to reinvent the wheel, so to speak, from its own inner resources. And here lies a surprising plot twist revolving around Gouzes chant and the ever-remarkable spiritual renaissances that periodically roll out of France.

Perhaps I can tell this story best from personal experience. In the

spring of 2000, I was on a three-week pilgrimage to France. Arriving in
Vézelay just before dusk, I climbed the steep hill to the grand old basilica
of Saint Mary Magdalene and spent half an hour or so wandering about,
enjoying its beauty. I had finished my tour and was on my way out through
a side chapel, when suddenly the sound of voices singing back in the
church caught my full attention.

What was *that*? It sounded like an angelic choir chanting some
strange, ethereal harmony—vaguely Byzantine, I thought, but with just a
hint of that distinctive Gallican flavor of southern France. I returned to
the sanctuary. There I saw a group of men and a group of women in blue
habits chanting the evening office. The women's heads were covered with
long white scarves, and both men and women were fairly glowing with fervor and joy as they knelt on their prayer stools. But it was the chant itself
that particularly arrested me; I had never heard anything quite like it before. I found the community's gift shop a block or so down the Rue Saint
Étienne and bought a CD. That was my first introduction to Gouzes chant
and the Fraternités monastiques de Jérusalem (FMJ).

The community itself is one of the fastest growing young monastic orders in Europe. In Shaker style, it consists of a men's house and a women's
house, with the sexes living under separate roofs but by a common rule as
they work side by side at their mission to be "the heart of God in the heart
of the City." They are part of an innovative experiment in urban monasticism, breathing new life into the dry bones of some of Europe's grand old
cathedrals through a meticulous and mystical chanting of the Divine Office. Barely thirty years old, the Fraternités monastiques de Jérusalem already have foundations at Saint Gervais in Paris, Mont St. Michel, and
Vézelay, as well as in Brussels and Strasbourg. The first North American
foundation opened in Montreal in 2004, and a new house will open in
Rome in the fall of 2006. Plans are currently under way for additional
foundations in Cologne and Poland.

The movement had its beginnings in the student riots of 1968 when

Pierre Marie Delfieux, the young chaplain at the University of Paris, recognized that the outcry he was hearing was not simply a political statement but a spiritual one. Life in the city had become too sterile and isolating. He began to envision a new form of monasticism that would be a visible spiritual presence at the heart of the secular city. When he shared his vision with his friend Cardinal Marty, the archbishop of Paris, Marty was sufficiently intrigued to send Delfieux into the African desert for two years to be spiritually formed in the footsteps of that great early twentieth-century desert hermit, Charles de Foucald. While there, the young Delfieux also formed a friendship with Carlo Caretto, another outstanding contemporary desert hermit and spiritual mentor. Upon Delfieux's return to Paris, his vision still untarnished, the bishop gave him Saint Gervais, an imposing but rundown old church on the banks of the Seine not far from Notre Dame. In short order, the worship at Saint Gervais was flourishing, and the new monastic community was growing by leaps and bounds.

The convergence of the Fraternités monastiques and Gouzes chant is another of those happy synchronicities, like Jacques Berthier and the Communauté de Taizé. Gouzes chant takes its name from André Gouzes, a brilliant and highly unconventional Dominican priest and composer who prefers to avoid the beaten track both musically and geographically. Gouzes hails from the Aveyron—the ancient Langeudoc of the Cathari and the troubadours—where the music has its own colorful history and flavor. In the early Middle Ages, Languedoc and neighboring Moorish Spain had each developed their distinctive traditions of sacred chanting, known respectively as Gallican and Mozarabic chant.[6] These two indigenous traditions gradually died out during the later Middle Ages, but their harmonies still linger in the air of southern France. Influenced by his own musical roots, as well as his deep love for the Byzantine liturgy of the Orthodox Church, Gouzes began a quarter of a century ago to create a comprehensive new repertory of chants for the Mass and Daily Office.

The two halves of the puzzle inevitably converged: a young monastic order in search of a means to solidify its liturgical practice, and a new body of chants looking for wider circulation. Over the past two decades, this symbiosis has had powerful reverberations. Gouzes chant has catapulted the FMJ into a prominence it would probably not have attained apart from its distinctive musical trademark. And as the order grows, it carries Gouzes chant right along with it.

MORE THAN MEETS THE EYE

Gouzes chant is classic psalmody—a new way of singing the traditional words of the Mass and Divine Office, not a re-visioning of the liturgy itself (as with Taizé). The chants are almost entirely in French, and Gouzes psalmody is at this point still a Francophone movement, although an English translation is presently in preparation by Brother Bradford Wolcott, the American-born prior of the FMJ community in Strasbourg.

On a first hearing, Gouzes chant can sound deceptively straightforward, as if the choir is merely singing simple harmonic progressions. But one soon realizes that these "simple" progressions do not emanate from a northern European harmonic base (as with Taizé). Instead, they echo the modal system of Byzantine chant and the pentatonic flavor of much of Near Eastern and Islamic chant; in fact, they sometimes echo them simultaneously, for Gouzes can marry these two distinct musical color palettes with astonishing effectiveness. The most striking musical signature of Gouzes chant is that the voice parts tend to operate in close harmony, with frequent accidentals and dissonances.

Listen to track 39 on your CD for a taste of the harmonic richness and complexity underlying this seemingly simple chorale from the Good Friday liturgy: [CD track 39] ⊙

O Christ, tu t'a - vances vers ta pas-sion vo - lon - tai - re

Bé - ni sois - tu qui viens au nom du Sei - gneur!

Ho - san - na au plus haut des cieux!

(O Christ, you advance toward your Passion by your own
choice. Blessed may you be, you who come in the name of the
Lord. Hosanna in the highest.)

This complexity throws us back, of course, into the familiar conundrum: the more subtle the art form, the less accessible it generally is for
congregational participation. The FMJ community struggles with this
dilemma. At Saint Gervais, where the emphasis is on maximum inclusivity, the singing is not as accurate as at Vézelay, whose prior (a former

actor) keeps the choir well rehearsed and transforms the Divine Office into high art. Bur even at Vézelay, the chants are simple enough that the thousands who now throng the church for Holy Week can pick up the basic tunes and sing along with gusto and passable accuracy.

And sing along they do. Whether in Vézelay, Mont St. Michel, Paris, or Strasbourg, thousands have shared the same experience I had; walking into what they thought was merely a tourist attraction and exclaiming, "What was *that?*" when the sound and sight of vibrant spiritual community touched their hearts. Père Delfieux's vision of "the heart of God in the heart of the city" has succeeded beyond perhaps even his wildest imaginings. At Saint Gervais, the mother house, a large extended community now regularly joins the FMJ for evening prayer. People arrive from work, set down their briefcases, pick up a choir book, and join in chanting the office. In the back row of the monastic choir, there are usually half a dozen or more new postulants eager to sign on. Whether the momentum will sustain itself is hard to tell, but the young order has definitely made a strong beginning.

Well ensconced in his small monastic outpost at Sylvanès, near Rodez, André Gouzes continues to labor toward the completion of his life's work: a comprehensive codex of settings for the Mass and Divine Office (including the complete Psalter) and special liturgies for the entire Christian year. His *Messe de Rangeuil* is already in widespread use in Europe.

Gouzes psalmody has yet to be widely discovered in North America, and until an English-language version becomes readily available, it will likely remain a specialty practice. But its musical genius is already well attested in Europe. (If you're traveling to France, definitely don't miss it!) Through a unique and subtle combination of musical elements, Gouzes has created a powerful new vehicle to convey the timeless beauty of Christian chant and psalmody. What's even more interesting (to me, at least) is that this beauty has proved in and of itself to be a catalyst for the revival of monastic life, the two bootstrapping each other toward new expressions of spiritual vitality. There may yet be life in what is too soon presumed to be a dying art form: classic monasticism built around the core practice of chanting the psalms. Who knows? After three thousand years of continuous operation, the spiritual legacy of psalmody may prove to hold a few secrets that reason alone cannot unfold.

18

DANCING
before
the ARK

I N THE OLD TESTAMENT book of Samuel, there is a vivid story of how
King David, triumphantly returning Israel's sacred Ark of the
Covenant to Jerusalem after decisively routing the Philistines, was so
overcome with ecstasy that he stripped to his loincloth and danced before
the ark.[1] The words of this ancient tale go as follows:

> So David went down and brought up the ark from the House of
> Obed-Edom to the city of David with rejoicing. When those
> who were carrying the ark of the Lord had taken six steps, he
> sacrificed a bull and a fatted calf. David, wearing a linen ephod
> [loincloth], danced before the Lord with all his might while he
> and the entire house of Israel brought up the ark of the Lord
> with shouts and the sound of trumpets. (2 Samuel 6:12–15)

Such displays of exuberance make some people intensely uncomfort-
able—both three thousand years ago and today. David's wife, Michal, was

one of these people: "When she saw King David leaping and dancing be-fore the ark," the story records, "she despised him with all her heart" (2 Samuel 6:16). But David responded to her upbraid with justly immortal-ized words: "I will celebrate before the Lord."

 ## The Psalms Personified

With good reason is David acclaimed and loved as the father of the psalms. While we've seen that this ascription is only partly true histori-cally, it is one hundred percent true emotionally, for his spirit throbs through the songs, and this vivid incident before the ark is essentially an icon of all I've been saying about the psalms throughout this book. If you sit with the story deeply, you'll see that it beautifully captures all three as-pects of what I've described as "the hidden wisdom of psalmody." It pin-points the source of the psalms' enduring energy and creativity. And it at least partially explains their surprising efficacy as the leaven in the dough of contemplative transformation.

First of all, David is passionate, and so are the psalms. Remember how in chapter 5 I quoted the Desert Father John Cassian as saying that the psalms carry within them "all the feelings of which human nature is capa-ble"? The real passions in life run strong and deep. When David is over-joyed, he doesn't hold back; he throws himself soul, mind, and body into the dance of ecstasy before his God. The psalms do this as well and en-courage us to follow suit. Emotion runs strong in the psalms and with huge mood swings. There is joy and crushing defeat, hope and bitterness, exu-berance and tenderness, grief and celebration—all swirling together in the messy, pulsing reality that is life. The psalms encourage us to dive deep and swim deep, acknowledging the reality of our emotional life as the place where spiritual transformation really happens. The religious path, gen-uinely embraced, is not a place for bystanders and backbiters. It is a sea we must swim in deeply if our hearts are ever to come to their final integration. For nearly three thousand years, the psalms have held up the mirror to the sacred reality of our human journey in all its seething untidiness. In the apt words of contemporary philosopher Jacob Needleman, they do not allow us to "make a religion of our better moments."[2] They encourage us to engage honestly and fully with the power and profundity that is life itself. Like David, they are a life force calling us to the dance.

Second, David's response to this life force is through his creativity. When moved to the core, he doesn't just yell and jump; he dances. The passion of his heart is transformed into a sacred art form that gives shape and direction to his emotions. The psalms are like this too, both in what they are and in what they touch off inside us. In and of themselves, they are already creative responses to the power and passion of the divine presence. But as we've seen throughout this book, the psalms also seem to have a catalytic effect, spawning their own domino-like chain of creativity. From the ancient Celtic psalters to the exquisite illuminated breviaries of the Middle Ages, from the seafaring legends of Saint Brendan to the sculpture and stained glass of the great medieval cathedrals, from the sublime artistry of Gregorian chant to the continuing artistry of Taizé and Gouzes chant: peel back the surface of Western sacred art and at the core you'll likely find the psalms. Their innate creativity seems to set other creativity in motion.

We've looked closely in this book at why this is so. The psalms have traditionally been entrusted, in Christian monastic practice, with the training of the unitive imagination. The unitive is that deeper, luminous vision in each of us that can perceive the world as meaningful pattern and synchronicity, that knows how to "see heaven in a grain of sand." The psalms have been the spiritual bridle and reins guiding the journey from the literal level of scripture into those deeper pathways of the christological and allegorical imagination. Ultimately their destination is the unitive state wherein, as Cassian observes, "We sing the psalms as if we've composed them!" Like Saint Brendan, we begin to live in two worlds simultaneously: an outer world of time and place and an inner world of meaning, coherence, and beauty. When the two come fully together, that is the attained unitive life. Then we begin to live and love our life for the psalm that it is: our own unique dance before the Ark.

Contemporary neurological scientists are paying increasing attention to the accumulating evidence that contemplative spiritual practice actually repatterns the neural pathways of the brain. The traditional monastic desideratum of putting the mind in the heart is now finding literal confirmation as scientists discover an intricate brain-heart feedback loop that can respond to external stimuli with vastly enhanced creativity and flexibility.[3] The ancient monks may not have had the language or the scientific equipment, but they seemed to know instinctively that their intensive contemplative work with the psalms had something essential to do with opening up this far more creative inner circuitry. Since the time of Saint Benedict, the Divine Office and chanted psalmody have been the unacknowledged chief instruments for this monastic neural repatterning. It is hardly surprising that their legacy in time and space has been a virtually boundless creativity.

Finally, David is naked—or virtually so. Stripping off his regal battle armor, he dances clad only in a loincloth, exposing fully to God who and what he is. We have seen how this, too, has been one of the chief features of the psalms as they've been used in contemplative practice. Through a process described by Thomas Keating as "the purification of the unconscious," they strip away our psychological battle armor and invite (in fact, impel) us to dance naked before God, revealing our shadow and wounds: our undigested anger, self-pity, and vindictiveness, those dark places we would prefer to keep hidden. We have looked at how the psalms, chanted in community as the backbone of the Daily Office, have furnished a common liturgical vessel both for acknowledging the shadow side and for releasing it.

David is well aware that the process is painful. In response to Michal's criticism, he acknowledges, "I will become even more undignified than this and I will be humiliated in my own eyes" (2 Samuel 2:22). But he realizes that this vulnerability and self-exposure is the flip side of his passion and creativity: it's what allows the authenticity of the life force to manifest. The psalms, like David, commit themselves to this full exposure and healing of the human person. That is why, as we saw in chapter 4, even the most violent cursing psalms, when used within the context of contemplative practice, contribute to the healing and gentling of our being.

"The psalms are your path; never leave it," Saint Romuald wrote in the eleventh century. For nearly two thousand years, Christian monastic practitioners have sensed in these 150 clay vessels the hidden treasure of their own transformation. While lacking the inclination or the psychological language to discuss the process in detail,[4] they at least had the spiritual sense to stay close to the living waters.

PSALMODY AND THE SECOND AXIAL

What of our own era? I have remarked many times in this book on the ferment touched off at Vatican II when the Catholic Church shelved its thousand-year-old tradition of Latin Gregorian chant in favor of new experiments in the vernacular. Before then, Gregorian chant and psalmody were a monolithic tradition. Now it's a whole new ballgame. For the first time in Christian experience, chant and psalmody have come slightly unglued. There are new forms of chanting that do not make use of the psalms at all or at least do not use them in the traditional way. Nowadays you'll often encounter the psalms in the form of brief antiphons and mantras intended to facilitate the entrance into contemplative prayer and meditation, rather than in their traditional role as the second rung— moral purification—on Simeon the New Theologian's classic ladder of spiritual ascent.[5] In this new format, they bring Christian tradition much more closely in line with universal traditions of sacred chanting. They are certainly easier to manage and teach, requiring less cerebral engagement and a lot less rehearsal time.

There are some who would say this is a sign of the times, which may in fact be true. The psalms are Israel's supreme contribution to the axial period. Worldwide, this era (approximately 800–200 B.C.E.) marked the dawn of personal conscience and accountability; through an apparently spontaneous quantum leap of human consciousnenss, it gave rise to the present family of world religions, whose foundation is the salvation (or enlightenment, depending on which side of the globe you come from) of the individual soul. The individual is the chief operative in axial consciousness. The psalms champion and celebrate this sense of individual relatedness; it's the heart of what they're all about. Again, like David dancing before the Ark, they celebrate the unique human being in a passionate, conscious relationship with God.

Three millennia later, there are many who feel that civilization is at the dawn of a new axial period. There is some emerging agreement as to what this new consciousness looks like: less grounded in the mental egoic perception that sustains our usual sense of selfhood; less dualistic and boundaried; more attuned to a new collectivity where each of us (like individual snowflakes) derive our full meaning and splendor from the whole (the snow). Visionary philosophers such as Ken Wilber, Wayne Teasdale,[6] and His Holiness the Dalai Lama have attempted to describe and nurture this emerging consciousness.

What does that do to the tradition of psalmody? "New wineskins for new wine," some would say. Just as the psalms were a unique flowering of that first axial consciousness, so the new consciousness will create its new art forms, if not its new religions. Imaginative new expressions such as Taizé chant and the Songs of the Presence seem like steps in the right direction toward a universally inclusive experience of sacred chanting that will honor the common ground in all seeking hearts and offer a strong new starting point for the celebration of unitive personhood.

All of this may well be; as yet, I have no firm opinion on the matter. I love the participatory beauty of the new simplified chant forms and the spiritual depth and unity they so brilliantly evoke. And I acknowledge the challenges involved for modern men and women in chanting the psalms with sufficient depth and consistency that their purifying alchemy is actually engaged. For to live with the psalms honestly and fully means making a commitment to ingest them honestly and fully, and this practice admittedly requires a certain investment of time.

Yet, as these thoughts swirl through my mind, I sit down morning and evening and chant my psalms. I have been doing it for so long that Saint Romuald's reminder that "the psalms are your path; never leave it" is no longer a marching order, just the description of how I've lived my life. I *haven't* left this path; it's been the one rock-solid piece of my spiritual practice through thirty years of internal and external adventuring. Yes, I've spent my share of time daydreaming and simply putting in the motions. But every so often—particularly in recent months—as I chant these familiar words, I sudddenly seem to be waking up to whole new subtleties of meaning, both in them and in my own life, and to occasional shafts of an unmistakable golden tenderness that reminds me that I am indeed in the Presence. Like King David, there are more and more of those days when I want to simply strip down and dance before the Ark; perhaps that's what I'm actually doing inwardly while outwardly the cat lies curled on my lap.

Be that as it may, I take joy that these old friends have been in my life and I in theirs. Like that unknown Irish monk in chapter 5, I give thanks for these "mighty melodies that throughout the world resound." And to Père André Gouzes (whom I've never met) and those glowing young souls in the Fraternités monastiques de Jérusalem, I send my heartfelt gratitude for demonstrating that these ancient songs sung anew can and do continue to bear the weight of our postmodern spiritual yearning. Where "the heart of God in the heart of the city" glows brightly, there the psalms continue to find their place.

Notes

Introduction

1. Kathleen Norris, *The Cloister Walk* (New York: Riverhead, 1996).

Chapter 1: The Psalms of Ancient Israel

1. Of course, there is a certain circularity built into this assertion. The Gospel writers remember Jesus as speaking through the Psalms; whether he actually did so or whether this is a memory preserved through the fledgling Christian church will probably never be settled with certainty. But since the collective memory of tradition is one of the most powerful ways in which knowledge of Jesus has been handed down, it makes the most sense simply to receive it as a true memory and work within its givens. As Father Theophane recognized, it has certainly been foundational to Christian contemplative spirituality.

2. The numbering, of course, came after the fact and with a certain amount of disagreement between the two main streams (the Hebrew and the Greek) through which the psalms were transmitted to the Christian West. As a result, Roman Catholic usage (which until very recently followed the Greek version) and Protestant usage (which follows the Hebrew) tend to be off by one in their numbering throughout most of the Psalter. For more on this, see chapter 6.

3. Psalm 137, for example, which laments the "Babylonian captivity," or the forty years the people of Israel spent in exile in Babylon (modern day Iraq) (586–546 B.C.E.), would obviously have to have been written during or not too long after this watershed event in Israel's history.

4. Leopold Sabourin, *The Psalms: Their Origin and Meaning* (Staten Island, N.Y.: The Society of St. Paul, 1969), 1:2.

5. Karl Jaspers, *Vom Ursprung und Ziel der Geschicte*, trans. Michael Bullock in *The Origin and Goal of History* (New Haven, Conn.: Yale University Press, 1953). Quoted in Ewert H. Cousins, *Christ of the 21st Century* (Rockport, Mass.: Element, 1992), 5.

6. Ken Wilber, *Up from Eden* (Boston and London: Shambhala Publications, 1982). Wilber's work builds on the groundbreaking insights of Ernst Neuman, an early disciple of Karl Jung, in his book *Art and The Creative Unconscious* (New York: Harper & Row, 1959).

7. John Cassian, *Conferences*, trans. Colm Luibheid (Mahwah, N.J.: Paulist Press, 1985), 133.

8. This term comes from Father Thomas Keating, who has made extensive use of Wilber's paradigm in developing his own teaching on "The Divine Therapy." See Cynthia Bourgeault, *Centering Prayer and Inner Awakening* (Cambridge, Mass.: Cowley Publications, 2004), 96–8.

Chapter 2: Early Monastic Psalmody

1. See particularly Benedicta Ward, trans., *The Sayings of the Desert Fathers* (Kalamazoo, Mich.: Cistercian Publications, 1984); Armand Veilleux, ed., *Pachomian Koinonia*, 3 vols. (Kalamazoo: Cistercian Publications, 1980–1983). The original, and in some ways still the best, of the early translations is Thomas Merton, *The Wisdom of the Desert* (New York: New Directions, 1964).

2. Ward, *Sayings of Desert Fathers*, 64

3. John Cassian, *Conferences*, trans. Colm Luibheid (Mahwah, N.J.: Paulist Press, 1985), 133.

4. "The Brief Rule of Saint Romuald," displayed at the retreat house at New Camaldoli Hermitage, Big Sur, California.

5. By far the most extensive and informative edition of this foundational spiritual text is *The Rule of St. Benedict* (Collegeville, Minn.: The Liturgical Press, 1980).

6. *Rule of St. Benedict*, 215.

7. The term *monk*, from the Latin *monos* or "single one," properly includes women monastics as well and is increasingly replacing the word *nun* to describe a female monastic.

8. James A. Walsh, trans. and ed., *Wisdom and Other Works by the Author of the Cloud of Unknowing* (Mahway, N.J.: Paulist Press, 1988), 221, 229.

9. *Rule of St. Benedict*, 217.

Chapter 3: Psalmody as Christian Yoga

1. Historical research designates at least four non-Gregorian parallels or antecedents to Gregorian chant: Ambrosian, Gallican, Mozarabic, and Old Roman. The ultimate source of all of these is believed to be Antioch or Jerusalem, emphasizing once again the continuity of Christian chanting with its Near Eastern and specifically Jewish roots.

   Present scholarship increasingly suggests that the association of Gregorian chant with Pope Gregory I is actually a misidentification. Gregorian chant is now thought to have originated as a reworking of Old Roman chant by Frankish cantors during the Carolingian period (eighth century). The association of the chant with the name of Gregory took place during this period and rests on an ascription copied into the early Frankish choir books from their Roman sources: *Gregorius presul composuit hunc libellum musical artes* ("Pope

Gregory composed the scores of these musical pieces"). There is reason to believe that the Gregory the Romans had in mind was Pope Gregory II (who was pontiff from 715 to 731), but the Franks assumed that it referred to the earlier pope. For more on this complicated subject, see *The New Grove Dictionary of Music and Musicians*, 2 ed., vol. 10 (London: Macmillan, 2001), 373.

2. For a further explanation of the meaning and importance of an arcanum, see Robert Powell, trans., *Meditations on the Tarot: A Journey into Christian Hermeticism* (New York: Tarcher/Putnam, 2002), 4.

3. *Rule of St. Benedict,* 229.

4. Alfred Tomatis, *The Conscious Ear: My Life of Transformation through Listening* (Tarrytown, N.Y.: Tarrytown/Station Hill, 1992).

5. The Cistercians (taking their name from the Citeaux, the monastery they founded in eastern France in 1092) are a twelfth-century reform movement within the Benedictine tradition that calls for a renewal and deepening of the contemplative life. A further reform movement, centered at La Trappe in the seventeenth century, resulted in the Order of Cistercians of the Strict Observance (OCSO), or Trappists, as they are more commonly known. The oldest and best known of Trappist monasteries in the United States is Gethsemani Abbey, immortalized by Thomas Merton in *The Seven Storey Mountain.* Saint Benedict's Monastery in Colorado also belongs to this order. All Trappists are Cistercians, but not all Cistercians are Trappists.

The transformational program of this very intense form of Christian monasticism is a quintessential expression of medieval "love mysticism," grounded in the biblical Song of Songs, particularly as expounded in the work of William of Saint Thierry and Saint Bernard of Clairvaux, Cistercianism's two most prominent mystical theologians. In essence, it attempts to harness the powerful energy of erotic love in the service of spiritual transformation by concentrating this ardor on a divine (rather than earthly) beloved. The actual technology (never written about publicly but taught to me somewhat allusively by two Trappist elders I had the privilege of working with closely), involved a brutal but remarkably effective formula of sexual abstinence, hard physical labor, fasting, and contemplative devotion concentrated through chanting in choir. Within this program, Gregorian chant (through its highly specific way of working with breath, vibration, and harmonic geometry or overtone) essentially functioned as the chief method of raising the sexual energy from the lower through the higher chakras, particularly into the heart chakra, which emerged as the mystical fruit of all this highly concentrated sexual energy and the seat of the "new man" entirely consumed in God. The end product of this particular path of transformation has a very distinct vibration, an intensity but also a gentleness that's reminiscent of the Mevlevi Order of Sufism.

Cistercianism is a monastic expression of courtly love (which is a product of this same era); hence the transformation of erotic love is centered on devotion to the Virgin Mary, who remains the patron saint of all Trappist houses and is honored in prayer as the final gesture of each monastic day.

6. Of course, the yoga of the choir isn't confined to choir practice alone; it spills over into every corner of the monastic life, just as the monks' daily work—when carried out with mindfulness and sensitivity to one another—significantly affects the quality of the chanting. They go hand in hand, carrying out that essential Benedictine template for transformation, *ora et labora*. This, incidentally, is the main reason that professional choirs, no matter how talented, never seem quite able to sing Gregorian chant with the same effortless grace as those monks at Saint Benedict's or Los Silos. The missing ingredient can't be emulated from outside; it is arrived at from deep within, from the life itself. No matter how impressive the vocal pyrotechnics, Gregorian chant sung by a secular choir always betrays itself by

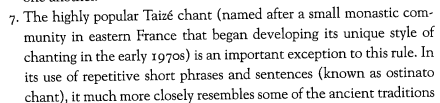
a slightly too sharp or pushy energy, like new wine that has not yet
had time to ferment. The deep bouquet of Gregorian chant is prayer
itself, emerging from the monks' common life of service to God and
one another.

7. The highly popular Taizé chant (named after a small monastic community in eastern France that began developing its unique style of
chanting in the early 1970s) is an important exception to this rule. In
its use of repetitive short phrases and sentences (known as ostinato
chant), it much more closely resembles some of the ancient traditions
of Near Eastern and Sufi chanting. I will have more to say about this
form of Christian chanting in chapter 15.

Chapter 4: The Psalms as Psychological Tools

1. Kathleen Norris, *The Cloister Walk* (New York: Riverhead, 1996).
2. Norris, *The Cloister Walk*, 95–6.
3. Ibid.
4. Norris, *The Cloister Walk*, 99.
5. Keating's teaching on the divine therapy is presented most fully in his
book *Invitation to Love* (New York: Element, 1992). For an overview
and critique, see chapters 9 and 10 in Cynthia Bourgeault, *Centering
Prayer and Inner Awakening* (Cambridge, Mass.: Cowley, 2004).
6. Norris, *The Cloister Walk*, 105.
7. Helen Luke, *Old Age* (New York: Parabola Books, 1987), 95.
8. Norris, *The Cloister Walk*, 101.
9. Ibid.

Chapter 5: The Psalms as Soul Music

1. The image of wine casks as a metaphor for the four senses of scripture
was first suggested by Alexander of Canterbury, a twelfth-century

Benedictine monk, in his commentary on a line in the Song of Songs (Psalm 2:4): "He brought me into his wine cellar." The entire passage is quoted in André Louf, "Scientific Exegesis or Monastic Lectio," *Collectanea* 22 (July–September 1960): 236ff.

2. Thomas Keating and most of the Trappist lineage prefer the schema: literal, moral, allegorical, anagogical (or unitive). The alternative, which I am using here—literal, christological, tropological (or moral), anagogical (or unitive)—flows more authoritatively from Henri de Lubac's magisterial work on the Christian liturgy, *Medieval Exegesis* (Grand Rapids, Mich.: Eerdmans, 1998) and is vigorously championed by the contemporary Camaldolese Benedictine monk and teacher, Father Bruno Barnhart. In fact, the order and even the number of these senses of scripture varied considerably throughout the patristic and medieval periods. For more information, see Simon Tugwell, *Ways of Imperfection* (Springfield, Ill.: Templegate, 1985), 93ff.

3. Thomas Keating, *Intimacy with God* (New York: Crossroad, 1994), 49.

4. Ibid.

5. *La Nature est un temple où de vivants piliers*
   Laissent parfois sortir de confuses paroles;
   L'homme passe à travers des forêts de symboles
   Qui l'observent des regards familiers.

   From "*Correspondances*" in Charles Baudelaire, *Les Fleurs du Mal* (Paris: Librairie Gallimard, 1951).

6. The most accessible modern translation is by John J. O'Meara, *The Voyage of Saint Brendan* (Buckinghamshire, England: Colin Smythe, 1991).

7. For an account of this adventure, see Tim Severin, *The Brendan Voyage* (New York: Avon books, 1979).

8. Philip Booth, "Heading Out," in *Lifelines* (New York: Viking Press, 1999), 199.

9. In James Carney, ed., *Medieval Irish Lyrics* (Dublin: Dolmen Press, 1967), 77.

 Chapter 6: Psalters and Sourcebooks

1. At least this is so for Protestant Christians. For English-speaking Roman Catholics, the comparable "authorized version" has been the Douay Version, a translation of the Latin Vulgate text which until the Vatican II reforms was the foundation of Catholic scriptural tradition.

2. For an excellent overview of the history of Bible translations, see *The Oxford Dictionary of the Christian Church* (London: Oxford University Press, 1974), 169–72.

3. *Christian Community Bible* (Quezon City, Philippines: Claretian Publications; Ligouri, Mo.: Ligouri Publications, 1995).

4. *The Living Bible* (Wheaton, Ill.: Tyndale House Publishers, 1971); *Good News Bible: The Bible in Today's English Version* (New York: American Bible Society, 1976).

5. *The Book of Common Prayer 1979* (New York: Church Hymnal Corporation, 1979). I am specifically referring to this more recent version, which was ratified in 1979 as the official Book of Common Prayer of the Episcopal Church. The earlier (1928) version uses the King James translation. The psalter can also be purchased separately: Gail Ramshaw and Gordon W. Lathrop, eds., *Psalter for Christian Worship: An Inclusive Language Revision of the Psalter of the Book of Common Prayer 1979* (Collegeville, Minn.: Liturgical Press, 1993). The United Methodist Church and United Church of Christ both include partial psalters in the back of their respective hymnals (based on the NRSV translation), along with the melodies for suggested refrains.

6. *The Psalms: An Inclusive Language Version Based on the Grail Translation from the Hebrew* (Chicago: GIA Publications, 2000).

7. Stephen Mitchell, *A Book of Psalms* (New York: HarperCollins, 1993).

8. Nan Merrill, *Psalms for Praying: An Invitation to Wholeness* (New York: Continuum, 1996).

9. Merrill, *Psalms for Praying*, vii.

10. Lynn Bauman, *Ancient Songs Sung Anew* (Telephone, Tex.: Praxis, 2000).

11. For more on this point, see Cynthia Bourgeault, *Encountering the Wisdom Jesus* (Boulder, Colo.: Sounds True, 2005). This is a six-CD audio teaching series.

12. This divergence gets even greater for a time with Psalms 114 and 115, which the Roman tradition calls 113A and 113B, but it catches up to the one-apart pattern again when the following psalm (116 in Protestant numbering) becomes 114–115 in the Roman Catholic usage.

Chapter 8: Suzuki Psalmody

1. Or you could sing, "For there is for**give**ness with you." But while my own sense of house style generally favors avoiding emphasis on a final pronoun, moving the cadence tone four syllables ahead in this particular case is so musically problematic that the better trade-off is simply to put up with the accented pronoun.

2. Those who are experienced in folksinging will probably also be familiar with the pentatonic mode, consisting of five successive whole steps. It is the basis of most of the great folk music traditions of the world, as well as many schools of sacred chanting.

3. For more on the subject of the medieval system of eight modes, consult *The New Oxford History of Music, Vol. 2* (1990), 2:110–12 or the *Liber Usualis*, xvii–xix.

1. We will consider in chapter 11 why this quick fix proves to be disappointing. In essence, part of the genius of Gregorian chant is that the medium and the message are welded indissolubly: the vowel-rich Latin language, the flowing melismas, and the fluid neumes and ligatures. Even inexperienced musicians, once they've been introduced to Gregorian notation, find it easier to sing Gregorian chant straight from the original than from modern musical notation. Unfortunately, the corollary holds equally true: the English language simply does not lend itself easily to the Gregorian visual format.

2. This boldface stanza is the doxology, a closing verse of praise for Father, Son, and Holy Spirit traditionally added to all Christian psalmody.

3. I put the word *measure* in quotation marks here and following because it really isn't. The term *measure* belongs to the world of mensural notation, where it designates one unit of whatever time signature the piece is written in (2/4, 3/4, 6/8, and so on). Since nonmensural chant doesn't have a time signature, the term is technically inappropriate. I use it here simply to designate a fixed visual unit of notational space and time.

4. A canticle is any piece of sacred poetry in either the Old or New Testament other than a psalm. As early as the Rule of Saint Benedict, the *Benedictus* was appointed as the canticle for lauds, where it follows the psalmody and scriptural reading and precedes the closing prayers. The *Magnificat*, or Song of Mary (Luke 1:46–55), holds a parallel position in the office of vespers. I will have more to say about these two canticles in chapter 10.

5. The Grail/Gelineau Lectionary Psalms for the entire liturgical year are available from GIA Publications in Chicago. For full information, see the bibliography at the end of this book.

6. During the 1990s, the Camaldolese monastic community systematically created its own body of psalm chants and notation. This ambitious work was primarily a labor of love by two talented monk-composers, Father Thomas Matus and Father Cyprian Consiglio. Before that, the Camaldolese Psalter, bound in blue three-ring binders, was the usual "cut-and-paste" arrangement of psalm tones from a variety of sources, including Gelineau in several notational styles.

7. Not exactly germane to the subject of this book, but worth mentioning in this regard is the psalmody of contemporary Anglican composer George Black, who has developed this "mix-and-match" strategy into a high art. His psalmody, geared more toward the parish choir than contemplative use, is available from ABC Publications in Toronto.

8. From *Lectionary Psalms*, 791. Note that this version is in harmony, as are most of the settings in this edition.

Chapter 10: The Wide World of Antiphons

1. Not to be confused with the word *antiphonally*, which as we saw in the last chapter, describes performance style based on alternating sides of a choir. There's a common thread between the terms, of course: the notion of "call" and "response." In antiphonal singing, one side of the choir is seen as answering the other. In similar fashion, the psalm itself responds to the call laid down by the antiphon.

2. The music for these antiphons is notated in a modernized Gregorian chant. The square notes correspond basically to quarter notes in modern notation. Some of the other neumes will be unfamiliar now, but I'll be introducing them in chapter 11.

3. I am not suggesting here a kind of "supersuccesionism," such as you'll sometimes find in Christian proclamations that Christ is the fundamental ground and that all other religions are really praying to him and through him whether they recognize it or not. The key to this

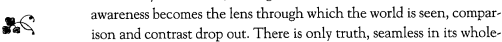

koan is actually simpler and much more accessible. The tendency to comparative thinking (which religion is the best?) is typical of, and fortunately limited to, the egoic level of awareness. Once unitive awareness becomes the lens through which the world is seen, comparison and contrast drop out. There is only truth, seamless in its wholeness. Thus, the problem of exclusivity, which dogs the heels of all three of the Abrahamic religions (Judaism, Christianity, and Islam), is really resolved not by changing the theology but by changing the lens of perception, by following any one of these particular paths all the way to its unitive endpoint. For me, this is the real meaning of the teaching "I am the way, the truth, and the life": "I am your path; walk me. When you arrive at where this path will lead you, you will see what your fractured mind cannot yet perceive: that all wholeness is One wholeness in the divine mercy."

4. For me, the most intriguing implication of Cousins's work lies in his observation that all of the major world religions have their roots in the first axial period—in other words, they herald and mirror the dawning of egoic consciousness, with its dual attributes of a personal sense of selfhood and a deep sense of separation. Within the context of these root perceptions, religion's primary function has been to contain, train, and moderate the shadow side of this consciousness while pointing beyond it to a transcendent Oneness that exceeds the limits of the egoic operating system. If, as many feel, humanity now stands at the edge of a universal second axial period, it may be that our present world religions, having served their role as stewards of the egoic, will be transformed into "new wineskins," disappearing in their present form to be reborn as appropriate vehicles for the manifestation of higher consciousness. InterSpirituality then becomes not so much about interreligious dialogue and tolerance as about a collective midwifing of the dawning new consciousness.

1. Sometimes you'll also see the punctum shaped like a diamond (its official name in Latin is *punctum inclinatus*), and sometimes you'll see it with a tail (in which case, it's called a *virga*). This combination is typically used in descending lines to suggest a grouping of notes with a slight accentuation of the first. This is one of the ways that Gregorian calligraphy gives important visual information about the subtle rhythmic innuendos of nonmensural chant. The actual "time value" of each note is the same: one pulse per note.

2. *Liber Usualis*, xxi.

3. *Liber Usualis*, xxiv.

Chapter 12: Customizing Your Psalmody

1. The first of these is a Gelineau tone. The second is obscure origin, but most likely the work of either Father Louis Coddaire, OSB cam., or Father Columba Kelly, OSB, of Saint Meinrad Archabbey.

2. Merrill's translation reads "all you who would serve the Divine plan." Throughout her book, she scrupulously avoids reference to God as the name of this Divine Presence. But "the Divine plan" does not point well to this or any of our other available psalm tones, so favoring musical sense over political correctness, I have opted for the G word.

Chapter 13: Developing Your Own Daily Office

1. The classic monastic psalmody for the little hours of sext and none involved working through portions of Psalm 119, that magesterial, 176-verse psalm considered to describe the ideal character of a monk. But the psalms in the 121–28 sequence (which are also represented in the Divine Office) seem much more relevant to the needs and concerns of contemporary lay contemplatives.

2. If these two-line verses can be combined gracefully into four-line units, then you can use any of the tones we practiced in chapter 12; they are all expressly designed to accommodate this line length.

3. A few communities—notably the Episcopal Order of Julian of Norwich and the Order of Saint Helena—make their psalters (complete with psalm tones) regularly available to the general public and encourage their lay members to participate in the daily chanting of the Divine Office. For specifics, see the musical resources section at the end of this book.

4. As a template for developing your personal Daily Office, an excellent resource to be aware of is Judith Sutera, *The Work of God* (Collegeville, Minn.: The Liturgical Press, 1999). This is a no-frills breviary, offering daily morning and evening prayers on a two-week cycle, with short scriptural passages and psalmody du jour. The very leanness of the translation makes these psalms somewhat hard to chant—they're haikulike in their simplicity. But for getting under way with a practice of contemplative psalmody when you simply have no time or inclination for complexity, this small volume can't be beat.

5. Remember that this will be the old-style Roman Catholic numbering system, which is generally one less than the numbering in a typical modern Psalter. Compensate accordingly. Refer to chapter 6 to refresh your memory on this technicality. Of course, Benedict's recommendations—geared to a weekly cycle and full-time resident monks—is far too ambitious for most contemporary lay practitioners, but it serves as a useful general guideline to the traditional order of psalmody.

6. I speak more about this tendency in chapter 10 of my book *Centering Prayer and Inner Awakening* (Boston: Cowley Publications, 2004).

Chapter 14: Is There Chanting beyond the Psalms?

1. In many of the great traditions, particularly Tibetan Buddhism, the chanting of sacred scriptures and bardos constitutes an important ele-

ment of practice, and these chants are every bit as elaborate and mentally rigorous as the corpus of psalmody. But this level of practice is not
typically made available to beginners; hence, many people in the
West are unaware of it.

2. Simeon the New Theologian, "Three Forms of Attention and Prayer,"
in E. Kadloubovsky and G. E. H. Palmer, eds., *Writings from the
Philokalia on Prayer of the Heart* (London: Faber and Faber, 1992),
159–60.

3. John Cassian, *Conferences,* ed. Colm Lubheid (Mahwah, N.J.: Paulist
Press, 1985), 133.

4. Those familiar with my work will know that I use the word *egoic* in a
much more limited and quantitative way than is typical in the tradition. I am not referring to selfishness or sinful self-will, but to our typical human perceptive mode (or "operating system"), based on
self-reflexive consciousness. By its sheer internal grammar, it inevitably divides the world into subject and object, inside and outside,
"me" and "them." The sense of selfhood generated through this operating system will thus appear to be a separate individual whose
uniqueness depends on a set of finite (meaning describable or deter-
minate) characteristics. Needless to say, this operating system, with
its inherent tendency to establish identity through the act of differ-
entiation (that is, separation) is the cause of a good deal of unnecessary misery and isolation and does indeed give rise to the sinful
self-will. But in and of itself, egoic selfhood is a question of perception, not morality. To attempt to purify the will without changing the
perception lands one in a painful double bind from which classic spiritual teaching (and much of contemporary Western psychology) has
suffered greatly. Egoic selfhood is not the foundation of personhood,
let alone consciousness; it is merely the view of the world generated
by egoic perception. Unitive perception generates a different and
far less anxiety-ridden sense of selfhood. For more on this, refer to

Cynthia Bourgeault, "Nurturing the Heart," *Parabola*, 27, no. 1 (2002): 6–12.

5. *The Rule of St. Benedict* (Collegeville, Minn.: The Liturgical Press, 1980), 217.

Chapter 15: Taizé Chant

1. Brother Roger Schutz, quoted by Jacques Berthier in his foreword to *Music from Taizé*, vocal edition G-2433 (Chicago: GIA Publications, 1978), iv.

2. Gelineau had worked with the community on an earlier project, translating the Divine Office into vernacular. Taizé was one of the places where Gelineau's method of singing the biblical text of the psalms to rhymical chants in harmony was first put into practice (and, in fact, the brothers still continue to sing the psalms in this way.)

3. For a recording of this chant and other selections in this chapter, consult the musical resources section at the end of this book.

4. All music and parts are available from GIA Publications. Consult the musical resources section at the end of this book.

5. While refrains and canons comprise the bulk of the music, the Taizé repertory also includes mass settings and acclamations (typically, alleluias, Kyries, and litanies, such as "Lord, hear our prayer"), and hymns. Thse all follow the basic pattern of cumulative repetitions, allowing the congregation to sink deeply into the beauty of the song, the deeply contemplative spirit, and the gathered presence of the community.

6. More recently, the Latin trend has begun to reverse itself as the community seeks maximum inclusivity by widening the number of languages in which the songs are chanted. Many of the most recent chants are in Russian and Slovakian, responding to the influx of Orthodox Christian pilgrims following the breakup of the Soviet bloc in 1989. Typically, vernacular chants will be offered in five or more lan-

guages; the particular version used depends on the congregation present. Currently, Taizé chants have been translated into forty-two languages worldwide, including Chinese, Hindi, and Zulu.

7. While most of the chants in the Taizé collection are based on an uninterrupted ostinato chant that goes on like the ebb and flow of the sea, there are a few exceptions. One of the most popular Communion chants, "Eat this bread, drink this cup," was originally conceived as an alternation between solo verses and choral refrain, more in the traditional style of a litany. But even this composition works perfectly well as an ostinato chant alone, minus the solo voices.

8. Production of the new songs at Taizé outpaces the ability of their U.S. publisher to keep up, and there are always a few songs that have not yet made it into the new GIA songbook. To be totally "au courant," you can order songbooks directly from Taizé, but the GIA collection is certainly more easily available and is entirely adequate to the purpose of most North American choirs and contemplative groups.

9. Christian Meditation is a classic form of mantric, or concentrative, meditation that works through the consistent repeating of a single mantra, or prayer phrase, typically *Maranatha* (Aramaic for "Come, Lord"). Centering Prayer is a looser form of surrender meditation, in which the mantra is repeated discontinuously: only when one becomes aware of being attracted to a particular emotion or thought. The two forms of meditation, though superficially similar, operate out of different transformational strategies and produce significantly different interior effects. For more on this, see chapter 3 in Cynthia Bourgeault, *Centering Prayer and Inner Awakening* (Boston: Cowley Publications, 2004).

Chapter 16: Songs of the Presence

1. Wisdom, comprehensively understood, is the art and science of integral spiritual transformation. It lies at the base of the great world reli-

gions and is reflected in the commonality of their spiritual practices, despite sometimes sharply divergent theologies. Practices such as meditation, nonattachment, and recognition of the illusion of the egoic self are all parts of a perennial template for transformation of the smaller, fearful, and violent self into the larger and more spacious one that is capable of genuine compassion and nonviolence. Contemporary Wisdom teachers and Wisdom schools seek to return to this integral model of transformation. For the Christian Wisdom teacher, Jesus represents first and foremost a master of Wisdom, calling his followers to exactly this deep and sustaining transformation of consciousness. Apart from such a transformation, his teachings are not only inpenetrable, but subject to dangerous distortion. For more on this point, see Cynthia Bourgeault, *The Wisdom Way of Knowing* (San Francisco: Jossey Bass, 2003).

2. Richard Rohr, *Everything Belongs* (New York: Crossroad, 1999) 54.

3. The CD is available for purchase from Praxis Institute at www.praxisofprayer.com.

4. In many schools of Islamic chanting, harmony is expressly forbidden because the purity of the unison line is thought to better symbolize the Oneness of God and of unitive experience.

5. This means reading the same passage two or three times, with an interval of silence (typically two to three minutes) in between. This allows the words to sink beneath the surface of the mind. Ringing a bell bowl at the end of each reading is a lovely ceremonial touch.

Chapter 17: Iona Chant and Gouzes Chant

1. John Bell, *Shorter Songs for Worship* (Iona, Scotland: Wild Goose Resource Group, The Iona Community; Chicago: GIA Publications, 1994), 11.

2. The conversion of England to Christianity was accomplished in two missions: one from Rome that landed in Kent in 597 and a second that brought Irish Christianity to Northumbria in 636 launched from Iona. The two strands of Christianity were distinctly different. Irish (Celtic) Christianity, remaining closer to its druidic roots, retained a much stronger sense of the feminine and of God embodied in the natural world. Moreover, due in part to the legendary exploits of the Irish sea-farers along the western Atlantic shores, Ireland received the heart of its Christianity directly from the Desert Fathers and Mothers of Africa, escaping the heavy Augustinian preoccupation with human sinfulness that affected the Roman Church. The Celtic tradition is quintessentially a Wisdom tradition, geared toward transformation and integration more than sin and penitence. The two strains of Christianity clashed sharply, not only on matters of doctrine and in-stitutional polity, but in their fundamental understanding of the Christian Mystery. While the English/Roman Church won the day at the Council of Whitby in 664, the Celtic tradition has survived as an underground stream. In contemporary times, Celtic spirituality has experienced a strong revival as men and women see it mirror their core concerns—a fuller integration of the feminine, a greater mutual-ity with the natural world, and a sense of delight in the here and now more than the otherworldly.

3. Bell, *Shorter Songs*, 11.

4. Ibid.

5. Bell, *Shorter Songs*, 88. For recordings of this piece and other songs from Iona, consult the musical resources section at the end of this book.

6. Mozarabic chant was actually fixed in place by the time of the Arab invasion of Spain in 711. But the Islamic presence in this region for the next three centuries, plus an active Jewish community that flour-

ished under Moorish rule, lent a distinctive Near Eastern flavor to the music of this region. For an excellent general introduction to Gallican and Mozarabic chant, see *The New Oxford History of Music*, vol. 2 (London: Oxford University Press, 1954), 2:72–91.

Chapter 18: Dancing before the Ark

1. For the ancient Israelites the most sacred symbol of their faith was the Ark of the Covenant, a golden tabernacle memorializing the covenant between Yahweh and his people. During a long siege of warfare with the Philistines, the Ark had been lost, regained, and sequestered in a series of temporary encampments. David's recapturing of Jerusalem made it possible to return the Ark to its rightful home. The full saga is told in 1 Samuel 4–7 and 2 Samuel 5–6.

2. Jacob Needleman, *Lost Christianity* (New York: Doubleday, 1980), 211.

3. Among the best general introductions to this burgeoning new field is Joseph Chilton Pearce, *The Biology of Transcendence* (Rochester,Vt.: Park Street Press, 2002). His Holiness the Dalai Lama has been so impressed by the evidence that he called a special conference in November 2005 to ponder the implications of this research in an interspiritual, prophetic context.

4. A marked reticence to talk about the physical technology of transformation is characteristic of Christian practice in general. The consensus is that revealing the technology runs the risk of creating skilled technicians rather than saints, people who can manipulate the mechanics of transformation to attain the desired ends, rather than entering through the straight and narrow gate of humility and inner poverty.

5. To review this schematic, see chapter 14.

6. Brother Wayne Teasdale was a brilliant missionary for interspiritual awakening. A student of both Thomas Keating and Bede Griffiths and a close friend of the Dalai Lama, he organized the Parliament of World Religions in Chicago in 1993 and in Barcelona ten years later. He died of cancer in October 2004. His most well-known book is *The Mystic Heart* (Novato, Calif.: New World Library, 1999).

Glossary

A CAPPELLA ("in the chapel style") When a musical composition is performed by voices alone, without instrumental accompaniment.

ALEATORY (aleatoric) Music in which an element of chance is deliberately built into the composition—either through passages left for improvisation, alternative sequencing, or different instrumental and/or vocal combinations—so that each performance is a new and partially random combination of variables.

ANGLICAN CHANT A distinctive form of liturgical chanting developed within the Anglican and Episcopal churches. While some of the chant is monophonic, its most characteristic form is nonmensural chant in four-part harmony. *See also* monophonic, nonmensural chant.

ANTIPHON A short, contrasting composition used to "frame" a psalm both musically and thematically.

ANTIPHONALLY A performance style featuring regular alternation between two groups of musicians; usually between two sides of a choir, but sometimes between a solo cantor and choir. In monastic psalmody, the psalms are typically chanted antiphonally.

ANTIPHONARY A book containing a collection of antiphons.

BENEDICT, SAINT (b. 480) The founder of Benedictine monasticism and principal shaper of the Divine Office, which has provided the basic template for monastic psalmody for more than fifteen hundred years. Benedict's teachings are preserved in the Rule of Saint Benedict, available today in many scholarly and popular editions.

BENEDICTUS Song of Zechariah (Luke 1:68–79), announcing the birth of John the Baptist. This beautiful New Testament canticle is traditionally appointed to the monastic office of lauds; its companion piece, the *Magnificat* (or Song of Mary) is sung at vespers. *See also* canticle, Divine Office.

BREVIARY A personal prayer book containing the readings, psalmody, and prayers of the Daily Office. *See also* Divine Office.

CADENCE TONE One of the three musical components (together with reciting and passing tones) of a psalm tone. It is the note that matches the final stressed syllable of any line of psalm text. *See also* cadence tone, psalm tone, reciting tone.

CANON A form of harmony created by singing or playing a single melody at different time intervals so that it harmonizes with itself. Also sometimes known as a round. "Row, Row, Row Your Boat" and "Frère Jacques" are familiar examples of the canon form.

CANTICLE Any scripturally based poem, other than a psalm, used in the liturgy of the Christian Church. The *Magnificat* (Song of Mary), *Benedictus* (Song of Zechariah), *Nunc Dimittis* (Song of Simeon), and *Te Deum* are the most important of the liturgical canticles, chanted at vespers, lauds, compline, and vigils, respectively. *See also* Divine Office.

CHOIR A word with overlapping meanings in Christian monastic tradition. It refers simultaneously to the *place* in the church where the monks gather to sing the Divine Office, the *people* who sing there, and the *practice* of singing itself as a devotional and transformational exercise.

CHURCH MODES *See* modes.

COMPLINE The last of the eight canonical hours of the Divine Office,
sung just before bedtime. *See also* Divine Office.

CONTEMPLATIVE PSALMODY The practice of chanting the psalms on a
regular and sustained basis, as the foundation of what has traditionally
been known in monastic terminology as the Divine Office. In this format, the psalms are absorbed deeply into the unconscious, where they
serve as the catalyst for confrontation and integration of one's shadow
side and the awakening of the unitive imagination.

CURSING PSALMS A name colloquially given to a number of psalms
marked by violent imprecations hurled against the enemy. Psalm 109
is the most notorious, but the tendency to villify the enemy is widespread throughout the psalms, causing some people to question their
political correctness and continued relevance as Christianity's premiere vehicle of liturgical prayer. For an extended consideration of
this topic, see chapter 4.

DAILY OFFICE *See* Divine Office.

DIVINE OFFICE (DAILY OFFICE) The comprehensive system of liturgical psalmody created by Saint Benedict in the fifth century as the
backbone of the curriculum in his "school for the Lord's service." The
phrase "divine office" is an English translation of the Latin *Opus Dei*,
or "work of God." For Benedict, the primary work of the monk was to
praise God in regular, round-the-clock services ("offices") anchored in
prayer and psalmody. He divided the twenty-four-hour day into eight
offices (vigils during the night, then lauds, prime, terce, sext, none,
vespers, and compline) and appointed psalms for each office in such a
manner that all 150 psalms were chanted in the course of one week.
Although the Divine Office has been shortened and simplified over
the centuries, it still serves as the foundation for most Christian
monastic and liturgical spirituality.

DOXOLOGY A short verse of praise for the Trinity traditionally added to all Christian monastic and liturgical psalmody. The classic words are "Glory be to the Father and to the Son and to the Holy Spirit, as it was in the beginning, is now, and ever shall be; world without end. Amen." (In Latin, it is "*Gloria patri et filio et spiritui sancto sicut erat in principio et nunc et in saecula saeculorum. Amen.*") In our more inter-spiritual and inclusive language–oriented times, you'll frequently hear variations on this formula—as, for example, "Glory to the holy and undivided Trinity, one God," or "Glory to God, Source of all Being, Incarnate Word, and Holy Spirit."

FIXED PSALMS Psalms appointed to a specific office for a specific day of the week, which do not vary from week to week or with the changing liturgical seasons. The "little hours" (prime, terce, sext, none, and compline) all have fixed psalms. *See also* Divine Office.

GALLICAN CHANT An indigenous form of nonmensural chant that grew up in southern France as early as the fifth century and for the next four hundred years provided the music for the ancient liturgies and monas-tic chanting of this region of France. This chant form died out in the later Middle Ages, as Catholic Christendom gradually was bent into conformity to the Roman rite and Gregorian chant. But echoes of the Gallican tradition can be heard in the contemporary liturgical chant of André Gouzes, a Dominican priest and composer from the Avery-ron in southern France. *See also* Gouzes chant, Gregorian chant, non-mensural chant.

GELINEAU, JOSEPH The founder of contemporary liturgical psalmody, Gelineau played a leading role during and after Vatican II in translat-ing the Catholic Church's Latin psalmody into the vernacular and providing simple, singable psalm tones to replace the Church's tradi-tional Gregorian chant.

GOUZES CHANT A contemporary chant form developed by André Gouzes, a Dominican priest from the south of France, combining ele-ments of Byzantine and ancient Gallican chant in a distinctive new musical art form. Gouzes chant has been popularized by its adoption within the Fraternités monastiques de Jerusalem, a young and rapidly growing French monastic order, as the basis for its liturgical psalmody. *See also* Gallican chant.

GRAIL PSALMS An English-language translation of Joseph Gelineau's original French translations of the Hebrew Psalms. The Grail Psalms, with their characteristic triple-stress rhythmic pattern, furnish the libretto for much of contemporary liturgical psalmody, particularly in the Roman Catholic tradition. *See also* Gelineau.

GREGORIAN CHANT The Roman Catholic Church's magnificent chef d'oeuvre, Gregorian chant furnished the music for the Divine Office for more than twelve hundred years, from its ascendancy in the early Middle Ages to its abrupt demise at the hands of Vatican II in the mid-1960s. While the chant is legendarily attributed to Pope Gregory I (540–604), present scholarship sees it as more likely the creation of Frankish cantors during the eighth-century Carolingian period. Fluid and melismatic, it leaves an indelible impression on all who hear it— and even more so, on all who chant it. While Gregorian chant is no longer the official music of the Roman Catholic liturgy, it has been enjoying an enormous popular revival, thanks in large part to CDs such as *Chant* (recorded live at the Monastery of Silos in Spain), which topped the pop charts about a decade ago. Contemporary seekers are increasingly respectful of both the aesthetic and transformative power of this unparalleled form of Christian yoga.

HOURS (canonical hours) A term traditionally used to describe the round-the-clock liturgical services comprising the monastic Divine Office. The "little hours" (typically short services with fixed psalmody) are prime, terce, sext, none, and compline; the "greater hours" (of greater length and complexity, and variable psalms) are vigils, lauds, and vespers. *See also* Divine Office, fixed psalms, variable psalms.

IONA CHANT (or Iona songs) A contemporary body of liturgical chants created primarily by Scottish composer John Bell and associated with the Iona community, a twentieth-century revival of monastic life on the venerable "holy isle" of Iona off the west coast of Scotland.

IMPROVISATIONAL CHANT Chant designed to give rise to spontaneous harmonic invention without a precomposed score.

LAUDS The second of the eight canonical hours in the monastic Divine Office, following vigils and intended to be sung approximately at sunrise. *See also* Divine Office.

LECTIONARY PSALMS Psalms appointed for use at Sunday public worship on a three-year cycle followed by the Roman Catholic and most mainstream Protestant churches. The lectionary psalms form the basis for most contemporary choral psalmody, including collections by Joseph Gelineau, George Black, Columba Kelly, David Haas, Richard Proulx, and others.

LIBER USUALIS A comprehensive (more than two thousand pages) collection of the Gregorian codex, containing Gregorian chants for the Mass, Divine Office, and special feast days for the entire church year, edited by the Benedictine monks of Solesmes and published (with introduction and rubrics in English) in 1956. *See also* Solesmes.

LIGATURE In Gregorian notation, several notes combined into one musical symbol.

LITTLE HOURS *See* hours.

LITURGICAL PSALMODY Psalmody chanted in communal worship as part of the Mass or theDivine Office.

LITURGY Any written and officially authorized service within a religious tradition; in a collective sense, the totality of these services. In Christian tradition, the principal forms of liturgy are the Eucharist (Mass) and the Divine Office.

MAGNIFICAT ("My soul magnifies the Lord") Canticle of the Virgin Mary

(Luke 1:46–55). This beautiful New Testament canticle is traditionally appointed to the monastic office of vespers; its companion piece,
the *Benedictus* (or Song of Zecariah) is sung at lauds. *See also* canticle,
Divine Office.

MANTRIC CHANTING Chanting a mantra or in a mantralike fashion
characterized by the continuous repetition of a short devotional
phrase or word.

MATINS An alternative term for the canonical office of vigils. In British
and Anglican usage, the term is commonly used to designate what
would technically be lauds, the service at or near after daybreak. In a
more general liturgical way, it simply means "morning prayer." *See also*
Divine Office, vigils.

MENSURAL CHANT A chant that has a regular, consistent beat and can
be transcribed in modern notation using a standard time signature.

MODES (church modes) Different ways of ordering a musical scale (ar-
ranging the sequencing of whole steps and half-steps within it), result-
ing in a distinctive musical color palette. In modern Western
harmony, major and minor modes are all that remain of a far more
complex system that guided the development of ancient and medieval
chant. Gregorian chant makes use of eight modes.

MONOPHONIC Music with a single melodic line that does not make use
of harmony.

MONOTONE CHANTING Singing on a single note.

MOZARABIC CHANT An early form of indigenous nonmensural chant associated with Spain, especially—after the Arab invasion of 711—
Moorish Spain. Like its counterpart, Gallican chant, it eventually
died out during the late Middle Ages as the Roman liturgy was universally imposed on Western Christendom. *See also* Gallican chant.

NEUMES The individual characters in the "alphabet" of Gregorian chant.

NOCTURN An individual liturgical unit within the office of vigils, consisting of psalmody and a scriptural or patristic reading, and separated from the next unit by a period of silence. Typically, vigils comprises three nocturns.

NONE The sixth of the eight canonical hours of the Divine Office, corresponding approximately to 3 P.M. (the "ninth hour"). *See also* Divine Office.

NONMENSURAL CHANT A chant that lacks a fixed meter or beat; its rhythm is determined by the natural flow of the words themselves. Also sometimes known as plainsong. Gregorian chant is nonmensural, as is much of contemporary liturgical psalmody.

O ANTIPHONS In monastic psalmody, a set of seven matching antiphons to frame the *Benedictus* and *Magnificat* canticles in the week immediately preceding Christmas. Each antiphon begins with the acclamation "O . . ." (*O Sapientia, O Adonai, O Radix Jesse, O Clavis David, O Oriens, O Rex gentium,* and *O Emmanuel*). In modern times, these seven acclamations have been combined to form the seven verses of the popular advent hymn "O Come, O Come, Emmanuel." *See also* antiphon, canticle.

OPUS DEI ("The Work of God") In Benedictine monasticism, the Latin name given to the practice of chanting the psalms in regular, round-the-clock worship services. Translated into English as "the Divine Office," this practice forms the backbone of the Benedictine monastic day. *See also* Divine Office.

ORA ET LABORA ("prayer and work") A phrase coined by Saint Benedict to express, as succinctly as possible, the Benedictine template for spiritual transformation.

ORGANUM A form of harmony produced by singing (or playing) a melodic line in exact parallelism a fourth below or a fifth above the original note.

OSTINATO CHANT A contemporary chant form developed by French composer Jacques Berthier, in association with the Taizé community, in which the congregation sings a simple, repetitive musical refrain (generally in two- or four-part harmony), which serves as the harmonic ground for more complex musical expansion in the accompanying instrumental and vocal soloists' parts. The repetitive chanting, which is mantralike in its effect, quickly draws the congregation into contemplative prayer, while the contrasting solo material provides musical diversity and beauty. *See also* Taizé chant.

PASSING TONE One of the three musical components (together with reciting and cadence tones) of a psalm tone. It is a note (or several notes) leading from the reciting tone to the cadence tone when the two are at different pitches. Each passing tone corresponds to a single unaccented syllable of the psalm text. *See also* cadence tone, psalm tone, reciting tone.

PENTATONIC Music based on a five-note scale consisting of consecutive whole steps. One of the most ancient of the modal systems, it is found in folk music worldwide.

PLAINSONG An alternative term used in the Christian liturgical tradition to designate monophonic, nonmensural chant, particularly Gregorian chant. *See also* monophonic, nonmensural chant.

POINTING The allotting of syllables in a psalm or canticle to the notes on which they are to be sung. While all musical notation is therefore technically pointing, the term more familiarly implies a kind of musical shorthand consisting of lines, slash marks, and dots ("points") above or below a syllable of text to jog the memory regarding where the changes in pitch occur.

PRIME The third canonical hour of the Divine Office, following lauds. *See also* Divine Office.

PSALM While the term technically applies to any hymn or sacred poem accompanied by a harp or other stringed instrument, it is commonly understood to designate the 150 sacred songs of the Old Testament Book of Psalms, the collected liturgical poetry of the people of ancient Israel.

PSALMIST A person who composes psalms.

PSALMODY The psalms in their dimension as a liturgical art form; particularly, the activities involved in working with the psalms in a devotional or transformational context: chanting, studying, and meditating on them.

PSALM TONE The melody to which a psalm is chanted.

PSALTER A book containing the psalms as a stand-alone collection.

RECITING TONE One of the three musical components (together with passing and cadence tones) of a psalm tone. It is a single pitch on which the majority of a line of psalm text is chanted. Only as the line approaches its final stressed syllable does the reciting tone give way to the cadence tone (sometimes moving through a passing tone to do so.) *See also* cadence tone, passing tone.

REFRAIN The part of a song that recurs at the end of each stanza. In contemporary liturgical parlance, sometimes used as an alternative term for *antiphon*, although the two are technically different. A refrain is an integral part of a song both musically and textually; an antiphon is a stand-alone composition used to "frame" a psalm or canticle. *See also* antiphon.

RULE OF SAINT BENEDICT A sixth-century monastic rule of life, attributed to Saint Benedict and governing all aspects of monastic conduct and spiritual practice. A product of earlier monastic tradition, it has furnished the template for Benedictine monasticism for more than fifteen hundred years. *See also* Benedict.

SALVE REGINA ("Hail, Holy Queen") A Latin hymn in honor of the Virgin Mary, traditionally sung in Trappist monasteries as the closing devotion of the day.

SCANSION Reading or speaking a line of poetry aloud in order to discover where its stressed and unstressed syllables fall. Since nonmensural chant takes its rhythm from the natural flow of speech, scansion is the necessary first step in pointing a psalm. *See also* nonmensural chant, pointing.

SEXT The fifth canonical hour of the Divine Office, corresponding approximately to midday ("the sixth hour"). *See also* Divine Office.

SOLESMES A French village near Le Mans which is home to the Benedictine monks of Saint Peter's Abbey. Since its founding in 1833 by Dom Prosper Gueranger, the abbey has become justly famous for its painstaking restoration of Gregorian chant. *See also Liber Usualis.*

SONGS OF THE PRESENCE A contemporary form of Christian sacred chanting being developed by a consortium of North American Wisdom teachers under the leadership of the Reverend Lynn C. Bauman. Inclusive in its lineage and outlook, this form of improvisational mantric chanting is broadly reminiscent of Sufi *zikr*, or "prayer of remembrance." *See also* improvisational chant, mantric chanting, *zikr*.

TAIZÉ CHANT A popular and influential new form of Christian contemplative chanting developed during the 1970s by the monks of the Taizé community in eastern France in collaboration with composer Jacques Berthier. *See also* ostinato chant.

TERCE The fourth of the eight canonical hours of the Divine Office, falling between prime and sext and corresponding roughly with 9 A.M.

TONE 1. A musical note or pitch. 2. The quality of sound made by singing—that is, by adding breath and resonance to the spoken word. 3. Synonym for a psalm tone, that is, a plainsong melody.

VARIABLE PSALMS Psalms appointed to a specific canonical office which vary from week to week or on some other regular cycle The "greater hours" (vigils, lauds, and vespers) all have variable psalms. *See also* Divine Office.

VERSICLE A single line (or half-verse) of psalm text, often designated in modern psalters by an asterisk (*) and used as the dividing point for antiphonal chanting. *See also* antiphonally.

VESPERS The seventh of the eight canonical hours in the monastic Divine Office, traditionally sung at sunset. Vespers is one of the "greater hours" of the Daily Office and is characterized by variable psalms and its own canticle, the *Magnificat. See also* canticle, Divine Office, variable psalms.

VIGILS The first and most complex of the eight canonical hours in the monastic Divine Office, traditionally sung in the middle of the night.

Bibliography

Psalters and Breviaries (text only)

Bauman, Lynn C. *Ancient Songs Sung Anew*. Telephone, Tex.: Praxis, 2000.

Book of Common Prayer 1979. New York: Church Hymnal Corporation and Seabury Press, 1979.

ICEL (International Commission on English in the Liturgy). *Psalms for Morning and Evening Prayer*. Chicago: Liturgy Training Publications,1995.

————. *The Psalter*. Chicago: Liturgy Training Publications, 1994.

Merrill, Nan. *Psalms for Praying, An Invitation to Wholeness*. New York: Continuum, 1996.

Mitchell, Stephen. *A Book of Psalms*. New York: HarperCollins, 1993.

Ramshaw, Gail, and Gordon W. Lathrop, eds. *Psalter for the Christian People: An Inclusive Language Revision of the Psalter of the Book of Common Prayer 1979*. Collegeville, Minn.: Liturgical Press, 1993.

The Psalms: An Inclusive Language Version Based on the Grail Translation from the Hebrew. Chicago: GIA Publications, 2000.

Sutera, Judith. *Work of God: Benedictine Prayer*. Collegeville, Minn.: Liturgical Press, 1999.

Bibliography

Brook, John. *The School of Prayer: An Introduction to the Divine Office for All Christians.* Collegeville, Minn.: Liturgical Press, 1993.

Endres, John C., and Elizabeth Liebert. *A Retreat with the Psalms: Resources for Personal and Communal Prayer.* Mahwah, N.J.: Paulist Press, 2001.

Le Mee, Katherine. *The Benedictine Gift to Music.* Mahwah, N.J.: Paulist Press, 2003.

———. *Chant.* New York: Bell Tower, 1994.

Merton, Thomas. *Praying the Psalms.* Collegeville, Minn.: Liturgical Press, 1956.

Norris, Kathleen. *The Cloister Walk.* New York: Riverhead, 1996.

Peterson, Eugene. *Answering God: The Psalms as Tools for Prayer.* San Francisco: Harper and Row, 1989.

Prévost, Jean-Pierre. *A Short Dictionary of the Psalms.* Collegeville, MN: Liturgical Press, 1997.

Sabourin, Leopold. *The Psalms, Their Origin and Meaning.* 2 vols. Staten Island, N.Y.: The Society of Saint Paul, 1969.

Sarna, Nahum. *On the Book of Psalms: Exploring the Psalms of Ancient Israel.* New York: Shocken Books, 1993.

Steindl-Rast, David. *Music of Silence: A Sacred Journey through the Hours of the Day.* Berkeley, Calif.: Seastone, 1998.

Books on Benedictine and Contemplative Spirituality

Bourgeault, Cynthia. *Centering Prayer and Inner Awakening.* Cambridge, Mass.: Cowley Publications, 2004.

———. *The Wisdom Way of Knowing: Reclaiming an Ancient Tradition to Awaken the Heart.* San Francisco: Jossey Bass, 2003.

Chittister, Joan. *Wisdom Distilled from the Daily: The Rule of St. Benedict and Modern Life.* San Francisco: Harper and Row, 1991.

de Waal, Esther. *The Celtic Way of Prayer: The Recovery of the Religious Imagination*. New York: Image Books, 1999.

———. *Seeking God: The Way of St. Benedict*. Collegeville, Minn.: Liturgical Press, 2001.

Hall, Thelma. *Too Deep for Words: Rediscovering Lectio Divina*. Mahwah, N.J.: Paulist Press, 1989.

Keating, Thomas. *The Mystery of Christ*. Rockport, Mass.: Element Books, 1987.

———. *Open Mind, Open Heart*. Rockport, Mass.: Element Books, 1986

Newell, J. Philip. *Listening for the Heartbeat of God: A Celtic Spirituality*. Mahwah, N.J.: Paulist Press, 1997.

Norris, Kathleen. *The Cloister Walk*. New York: Riverhead, 1996.

Pennington, Basil. *Lectio Divina: Renewing an Ancient Practice of Praying the Scriptures*. New York: Crossroad, 1998.

The Rule of St. Benedict 1980. Collegeville, Minn.: Liturgical Press, 1981.

Shapiro, Rami. *The Divine Feminine in Biblical Wisdom Literature*. Woodstock, Vt.: Skylight Paths, 2005.

Ward, Benedicta. *The Desert Christian*. New York: Macmillan, 1980.

Selected Musical Resources

Psalters, Scores, and Manuals

Bell, John. *The Iona Abbey Worship Book*. Iona, Scotland: Wild Goose Re-source Group, The Iona Community; Chicago: GIA Publications, 2005. Available at www.giamusic.com. G-6388.

————. *Come, All You People: Shorter Songs for Worship*. Iona, Scotland: Wild Goose Resource Group, The Iona Community; Chicago: GIA Publications, 1994. Available at www.giamusic.com. G-4391.

The Camaldolese Monks. *Lauds and Vespers*. Big Sur, Calif.: New Camal-doli Monastery, in press. For ordering information, contact: Book-store, New Camaldoli Monastery, U.S. Highway 1, Big Sur, CA 93920; 831-667-2456; monks@contemplation.com.

Carroll, J. Robert. *Guide to Gelineau Psalmody*. Chicago: GIA Publica-tions, 1979. Available at www.giamusic.com.

The Divine Office According to the Use of the Order of Julian of Norwich. Wausheka, Wis.: Order of Julian of Norwich, 2001.

Endres, John C., and Elizabeth Liebert. *A Retreat with the Psalms: Resources for Personal and Communal Prayer*. Mahwah, N.J.: Paulist Press, 2001.

Fowells, Robert M. *Chant Made Simple*. Brewster, Mass.: Paraclete Press, 2000.

Gouzes, André. *The Rangeuil Mass* and *A Sunday Vigil* are available in English editions. Various collections of psalmody are available in French, including *Le Psautier*, vol. 1; *Laudes*; *Vêpres*; *Psaumes & Eucharistie*. For a complete listing, visit www.sylvanet.org.

Kelly, Columba. *Lectionary Psalms for Advent and Christmas*. Chicago: GIA Publications. Available at www.giamusic.com. G-5256.

————. *Lectionary Psalms for Lent and Easter*. Chicago: GIA Publications. Available at www.giamusic.com. G-6056.

Lectionary Psalms: Grail/Gelineau. Chicago: GIA Publications, 1998. Available at www.giamusic.com. G-5040.

The Liber Usualis, with Introduction and Rubrics in English. Tournai (Belgium) and New York: Desclée & Cie, 1956.

The Saint Helena Breviary, Monastic Edition. Augusta, Ga.: Order of Saint Helena, 2005. Available from Office Manager, Order of Saint Helena, 3042 Eagle Drive, Augusta, GA 30916-5645; 706-798-5201; www.osh.org; orderofsainthelena@comcast.net.

Songs and Prayers from Taizé. Taizé, France: Ateliers et Presses de Taizé; Chicago: GIA Publications, 1991. Available at www.giamusic.com. G-3719A (accompaniment edition for keyboard, guitar, solo instruments, and cantor); G-3719-P (choral edition containing only the fifty chants).

Taizé: Songs for Prayer. Taizé, France: Atliers et Presses de Taizé; Chicago: GIA Publications, 1998. Available at www.giamusic.com. G-4956P (choral edition for the congregation); G-4956A (accompaniment edition for keyboard, guitar, solo instruments, and cantor).

Worship: A Hymnal and Service Booklet for Roman Catholics. 3rd ed. Chicago: GIA Publications, 1986. Available at www.giamusic.com.

Recordings

Note that CD = compact disc; CS = compact stereo cassette.

Bauman, Lynn C., with the Choir of All Saints Episcopal Church, Corpus Christi, Texas. *Songs of the Presence.* Telephone, Tex.: Praxis Institute, 2001. Available at www.praxisofprayer.com.

Bourgeault, Cynthia. *Singing the Psalms.* Boulder, Colo.: Sounds True, 1997. ISBN 1-56455-571-2 (3 audiocassettes, teaching series with enclosed psalm booklet). Available at www.soundstrue.com.

Day of the Resurrection: Liturgy of the Hours for Sunday. Big Sur, Calif.: New Camaldoli Publications and Tapes, 2001. Compact disc. For orders or information: Bookstore, New Camaldoli Monastery, U.S. Highway 1, Big Sur, CA 93920; 831-667-2456; monks@contemplation.com.

Gelineau, Joseph, and Alexander Peloquin. *Favorites of Gelineau Psalmody.* Chicago: GIA Publications. CS-211. Available at www.giamusic.com

Gelineau, Joseph, and Richard Proulx. *The Gelineau Psalms.* Chicago: GIA Publications. CS-122. Available at www.giamusic.com.

The Schola Cantorum of Saint Peter the Apostle, with J. Michael Thompson, dir. *Spirituality of the Psalms.* Collegeville, Minn.: Liturgical Press. CD: ISBN 0-8146-7952; CS: ISBN 0-8146-07953-6. Available at www.litpress.org.

Singing the Psalms. 4 vols. Portland, Ore.: Oregon Catholic Press. CD 10643GC (vol. 1); CD 10644GC (vol. 2); CD 10645GC (vol. 3); CD10608GC (vol. 4). Available at www.ocp.org

Fraternités monastiques de Jerusalem. *Exulte Jerusalem.* Compact disc. © Fraternités monastiques de Jerusalem, 2000. DBA-01-2000. Available at www.Jerusalem.cef.fr.

A Sunday Vigil—The Rangueil Mass. Compact disc. Kings College, London. Available through Les Publications de Sylvanès at www.sylvanet.com.

GREGORIAN CHANT

Chant. By the Monks of Santo Domingo de Silos, Spain. CD

Gregorian Chant. Schola of the Hofburgkapelle, Vienna. Compact disc. © The Musical Heritage Society, 1989. MHS 512365X.

Immortal Gregorian Chant. Part I (Advent, Christmas, Epiphany, Palm Sunday, Holy Thursday, Good Friday). Chicago: GIA Publications. CD-183, CS-183. Available at www.giamusic.com.

Immortal Gregorian Chant. Part II (Easter, Corpus Christi, All Saints, All Souls). Chicago: GIA Publications. CD-184, CS-184. Available at www.giamusic.com.

Monastic Choir of Saint Peter's Abbey, Solesmes. *Gregorian Sampler.* Brewster, Mass.: Paraclete Press. ISBN 1-55725-117-7. Compact disc. Available at www.paracletepress.com. Also available in boxed set with text and video from Multi Media Communications, 575 Madison Ave., New York, NY 10022.

IONA CHANT

Bell, John. *Come, All You People.* Chicago: GIA Publications. CD-355, CS-355. Available at wwgiamusic.com.

Bell, John, Mhairi Lawson, and The Cathedral Singers. *Psalms of David and Mary*. Chicago: GIA Publications. CD-403, CS-403. Available at wwwgiamusic.com.

TAIZÉ CHANT

Laudate Omnes Gentes. Chicago: GIA Publications. CD-575, CS-575. Available at www.giamusic.com.

Resurrexit. Chicago: GIA Publications, 1991. CS-169. Available at www.giamusic.com.

Songs and Prayers from Taizé. Chicago: GIA Publications, 1991. CD-226, CS-226. Available at www.giamusic.com.

Venite Exultemus. Chicago: GIA Publications. CD-529, CS-529. Available at www.giamusic.com.

Credits

Ladies of the Grail. Selected verses of Psalms 51, 57, 92, 96, 115, 143. © 1963, 1986, 1993, 2000, The Grail, England. Reprinted by permission of HarperCollins, Ltd. GIA Publications, Inc., exclusive North American agent, 7404 S. Mason Ave., Chicago, Ill. 60638. www.giamusic.com. 800-442-1358. Used by permission.

Chant settings of Psalm 138, O Antiphons, and the "Sixfold Easter Alleuia" used by permission of St. Benedict's Monastery, Snowmass, Colo.

Chant settings of Psalm 57, Psalm 63 (with antiphon), Psalm 100 (with Christmas and Easter antiphons), Psalm 143, Benedictus tone (no. 376) and Magnificat tone (no. 272). © 1994 Camaldolese Hermits of America.

Gelineau, Joseph. Chant settings of Psalms 51, 57, 92, 96. © 1987, 1998 by GIA Publications, Inc., 7404 S. Mason Ave., Chicago, Ill. 60638. www.giamusic.com. 800-442-1358. All rights reserved. Used by permission.

"There Is Nothing but God," "Slowly Blooms the Rose Within," "In the Name of the Holy One" © 2001 Praxis Institute, Elwood, Tex. Used by permission.

"Take O Take Me as I Am" © 1994, Wild Goose Resource Group, Iona Community, Scotland. GIA Publications, Inc., exclusive North American Agent, 7404 S. Mason Ave., Chicago, Ill. 6-638. www.giamusic.com. 800-442-1358. All rights reserved. Used by permission.

CD Contents

Index